The Baseball Trivia Quiz Book

Mitch "The Wild Thing" Williams and Dave Brown

Illustrated by Matt LaFleur
Foreword by Harry Kalas

Sterling Publishing Co., Inc.
New York

Library of Congress Cataloging-in-Publication Data

Williams, Mitch, 1964–
　　The baseball trivia quiz book / Mitch "the Wild Thing" Williams and Dave Brown; foreword by Harry Kalas ; illustrated by Matt LaFleur.
　　p. cm.
　　Includes index.
　　ISBN 0-8069-4472-2
　　1. Baseball—United States—Miscellanea. I. Brown, Dave. II. Title.
GV873.W55 2000
796.357'0973—dc21
　　　　　　　　　　　　　　　　　　　　　　　　　　99-087962

10　9　8　7　6　5　4　3　2

Published by Sterling Publishing Company, Inc.
387 Park Avenue South, New York, N.Y. 10016
© 2000 by David Brown and Mitch Williams
Distributed in Canada by Sterling Publishing
%0 Canadian Manda Group, One Atlantic Avenue, Suite 105
Toronto, Ontario, Canada M6K 3E7
Distributed in Great Britain and Europe by Cassell PLC
Wellington House, 125 Strand, London WC2R 0BB, England
Distributed in Australia by Capricorn Link (Australia) Pty Ltd.
P.O. Box 6651, Baulkham Hills, Business Centre, NSW 2153, Australia
Manufactured in the United States of America
All rights reserved

Sterling ISBN 0-8069-4472-2

Table of Contents

ACKNOWLEDGMENTS 5
PRE-GAME PRAISE FROM THE BROADCAST BOOTH *by Harry Kalas* 7
WARM-UP TOSSES *by The Wild Thing* 9

QUESTIONS

HANGING CURVEBALLS
Who Am I? 13
Mixed Bag   20
CHANGE-UPS AT THE LETTERS
Who Am I? 33
Mixed Bag 44
SLIDERS DOWN AND IN
Who Am I? 55
Mixed Bag 67
BLAZING FASTBALLS
Who Am I? 82
Mixed Bag.................................... 95

ANSWERS

HANGING CURVEBALLS
Who Am I? 110
Mixed Bag 110
CHANGE-UPS AT THE LETTERS
Who Am I? 113
Mixed Bag 114
SLIDERS DOWN AND IN
Who Am I? 117
Mixed Bag 118
BLAZING FASTBALLS
Who Am I? 120
Mixed Bag 121
About the Authors 125
Index 126

Acknowledgments

A tip of my hat goes out to a few dozen people who, in various ways, made significant contributions to my writing this book and getting it published.

The following folks are jointly credited with the win for enthusiastically taking my pre-Mitch quizzes over the years and urging me to write more; encouraging me to keep writing them even if they didn't know Mickey Mantle from Mickey Hatcher; and offering clutch suggestions on how to improve the book: my parents Bob and Nancy Brown, brother Doug (who was especially helpful in the final innings), sister Kristin Warren, her husband Fred, and their son Greg, cousin Leslie Henry, as well as friends Bob Anderson, Jim Anderson, Frank Ballew, Dave Beck, Rob Betts, Jim Blodgett, Dave Borghesani, Doug Brouder, Joe Brown, Jay Delduco, John Heron, Mike Jones, Steve Koons, Mike Krotman, Rick Kunkle, John Maney, Glenn Massey, Bill Mercer, Rob Neducsin, Mark Parsons, Jeff Rodimer, Dave Sautter, Steve Shebell, Gregg Siefert, Rod Smith, Scott Smith, Chip Staley, John Thompson, Paul Troy, Brad Vance, Greg Veith, and Mark Voigt.

These individuals collaborated to nail down the save: my longtime, hard-working legal secretary Helen Tarnacki (who occasionally would take a break from my work to do some book-related typing for me), my agent John Sammis (who made several important trips to the mound), lawyer Pat Thornton (who recorded some key late-game strikeouts), and the whole gang at Sterling, most notably editors Peter Gordon and Hannah Steinmetz and copywriter Susan Levitt, for their great work and for giving me the ball and letting me go the distance.

And finally, thanks to Mitch and his wife, Irene; this project would not have happened without their efforts, and for that they earned both a win and a save.

—*D.B.*

PRE-GAME PRAISE FROM THE BROADCAST BOOTH

What a great idea for a trivia book to include the insight and humor of "The Wild Thing."

Mitch Williams was an integral part of that wonderful, wacky bunch of Philadelphia Phillies, a team that in 1993 went from worst to first. It's a shame Mitch is remembered for the series-winning home run by Joe Carter. Almost forgotten were his 43 saves. The Phillies would not have been in the World Series were it not for their closer. Granted, of his 43, you could count on one hand the number of his 1–2–3 saves. "The Wild Thing" made it exciting...but he almost always got the job done. I remember walking into manager Jim Fregosi's office in San Diego before a day game, when Jim was still smoking. He had four packs of cigarettes stacked on his desk. I asked him if that was enough cigarettes to last him through the day. He retorted, "Not if Mitch pitches."

"Mitchie-pooh," as some of us called him endearingly, was zany away from the game, too. My late, great Hall-of-Fame partner Rich Ashburn always organized an eight-deck Blackjack game on our team flights. The stakes were $20 a hand and you could double-down anytime. When "The Wild Thing" played, if his first two cards equaled 12, he would always double. He coined the phrase "Double the Dozen."

With Mitch's baseball insight and humor, *The Baseball Trivia Quiz Book* makes for a provocative, interesting, and fun read.

—*Harry Kalas*

WARM-UP TOSSES
by The Wild Thing

Hi. *My name is Mitch Williams.* You may remember I was a hard-throwing, left-handed relief pitcher in the majors for 11 years. I broke in with the Rangers in 1986. I finished with the Royals in 1997. I helped Dykstra, Daulton, and the rest of the Phillies make it to the World Series in 1993.

All told, I saved 192 games in my career, and as my managers would tell you, practically every one was an adventure. Closers like Lee Smith and Dennis Eckersley, they would come into the game in the ninth and retire the side in order for a nice, easy save. How boring. I preferred the nail-biting variety. I'd come in with a one-run lead and usually start by walking the leadoff man. Get the second batter to fly out. Give up a single. Pop up the fourth hitter. Hit the next man to load the bases. My manager would pace in the dugout, getting grayer every minute, and send the pitching coach out to the mound to give me a pep talk. I'd run the count full on the sixth hitter of the inning. The runners would be off on every pitch, and the hitter would foul off two or three. Then I'd strike him out to end the game. Now that's a hard-earned save, isn't it?

That wildness of mine earned me my nickname. It happened in 1989 when I was with the Cubs. The movie *Major League* had just hit the screen. In case you haven't seen the movie, it's about a major league team in Cleveland whose owner wanted them to finish last so she could move them to Miami. They had this pitcher, Ricky Vaughn, played by Charlie Sheen, who threw hard but had some minor control problems. Like he uncorked four wild pitches in one inning. The fans dubbed him "The Wild Thing." Calvin Schiraldi, one of my teammates with the Cubs, thought there were some similarities between old Ricky and me (I can't understand why), so I became "The Wild Thing."

After retiring from baseball, I was running a bar/bowling alley in Pennsauken, New Jersey, with my father-in-law. A while back, this guy named Dave Brown from across the river in Philadelphia called me. He said he was a lawyer who used to write for *Inside Sports* magazine. *Oh brother,* I thought, *what a deadly combination—a guy who's a sportswriter and a lawyer. He'll probably misquote me and then turn around and sue me.* I was wrong, though. Dave turned out to be a pretty nice guy, and he really knew his baseball. He asked me if I'd be interested in co-authoring a baseball quiz book with him. He told me that he'd been writing these quizzes over the years entitled "Who Am I?" in which he described a player's career—what teams he played for, the number of home runs he hit, records he set, things like that—and he wanted me to spruce up the questions with funny stories and anecdotes about the guys I played with and against. No problem, I said. I've got an endless supply of those.

For example, take this relief pitcher who was on the Phillies with me. What a flake he was. Most relievers sit out in the bullpen, talking about how they'd pitch certain hitters if they got into the game that night. This deep thinker would be asking questions like "Why is it that we park on the driveway and drive on the parkway?" and "What was the best thing *before* sliced bread?" What kind of warped mind thinks up stuff like that?

Baseball players like to play practical jokes on each other, and I never missed the chance to get in on the fun. There was this outfielder I played with who skipped the minor leagues, so he wasn't introduced to practical joking until he got to the majors. Boy, was he an easy victim. I'd be eating an ice cream cone and I'd say, "Hey, buddy, this ice cream cone doesn't smell quite right. Will you take a whiff?" He'd say, "Sure." And, of course, I'd bury him with it.

And how can I forget that pitcher who had some rather unusual eating habits? We would be hanging around the clubhouse in the early innings before heading down to the bullpen. In the second inning, I'd see him make a phone call. "Who are you calling, your woman?" I'd ask him. "No, man. I just ordered a pizza." The list goes on.

Dave mixes in the more traditional trivia that I know you fans love, such as: What active player's father hit 332 home runs? Who are the only members of the 500 home run club that played their entire careers with one team? Name the only team that won a World Series in both the 1980s and 1990s. What pitcher in 1993 threw 55 straight innings without allowing a walk? I'll give you a hint on the last one—it's not me. I doubt if I ever threw 55 straight *pitches* without allowing a walk.

When Dave and I were finished, we had 200 questions. I felt like I had thrown both ends of a double-header after that. Forty percent of the questions are "Who Am I?" and the rest are a "Mixed Bag": some multiple-choice, matching, short answer—for a minute there, you're going to think you're back in school, except these questions are funny, entertaining, and thought-provoking. Take my word for it, you and your friends will have a great time trying to remember players like the Cubs' outfielder that sang the best National Anthem I ever heard and the starting pitcher on those 1993 Phillies who was as strong as an ox—and nearly as smart as one, too.

We're going to start you off with 50 "Hanging Curveballs." These questions are so easy, John Kruk could answer them—if he's not busy stuffing his face with food, that is. Next, we'll throw you 50 "Change-Ups at the Letters." You should be able to crank out a lot of correct answers to these questions, but be careful: If you're not ready for them, they might fool you. We get down to business in the next category when we toss you 50 "Sliders Down and In." You'll get to take your hacks trying to recall which one of my Rangers' teammates roomed with John Elway in college, and which was nicknamed "Sluggo" because he was so stinkin' slow. And then to close things out, we're going to rear back and throw 50 "Blazing Fastballs." These questions are so challenging, Bob Costas might be stumped on some of them.

"One more thing, Dave, we need a title for this masterpiece, don't we?"

"Yeah, I guess we do. What about *Baseball Bafflers by the Barrister and the Ballplayer?*"

"Could you try something that will fit on the cover?"

"Here's a nice, short title: *Brown's Baseball Brain Teasers.*"

"I thought you wanted this book to sell."

"Any ideas?"

"Look, you doggone lawyers think too hard about everything. It's really very easy. What is it that you know so much about?"

"Baseball trivia."

"And what is it that we wrote?"

"A quiz book."

"Put them together and what do you have?"

"*The Baseball Trivia Quiz Book*."

"No further questions."

Hope you enjoy the book.

—*Mitch "The Wild Thing" Williams*

HANGING CURVEBALLS

Who Am I?

1. As Mitch observed, people stand next to me and realize just how small they are. I'm six-foot-five, weigh about 245 pounds, and have arms as big as some guys' legs. Mitch used to have good luck with me when I was younger, as he struck me out often. For the most part, though, I've had my way with pitchers, especially lately. I hit 52 home runs in 1996 and came back in 1997 with 58 long balls. In 1998, I matched that figure by September 2, and then, under the glare of the national spotlight, thrilled the baseball world by adding a dozen more the last three and a half weeks of the season. I cooled off in 1999 and only hit 65 homers. Who am I?

2. I have a brother who is an identical twin, but our careers are hardly identical. He played in just 24 games with the A's and Cardinals in the early 1990s. On the other hand, I, who am bulkier than my brother, won the American League MVP in 1988 when I belted 42 home runs, drove in 124 runs, and added 40 stolen bases for good measure. I pounded a league-leading 44 home runs in 1991, but didn't win the MVP. I've been on the disabled list a lot in recent years (seven times since 1993), but still have racked up my share of homers—I hit a career-high 46 in 1998 and slugged 34 in 1999, even though I missed almost one-third of the season. Who am I?

3. Stan Musial, Robin Yount, and I are the only players who rank first all-time for a franchise in singles, doubles, triples, and home runs. In my long and distinguished career, I amassed 2035 singles, 665 doubles, 137 triples, and 317 home runs, for a total of 3154 hits, which earned me induction into the Hall of Fame in 1999, the first year that I was eligible. Home run number 200 came off Mitch in his rookie campaign of 1986, after he had been misquoted in my team's local newspaper. The Rangers were coming to town and one of the writers who covered my team asked Mitch how he felt about facing me for the first time, and he answered, "The rumor is that I'm wild and I throw hard, so he might not be too comfortable in there his first at bat." The paper twisted Mitch's words and printed a headline the next day which said that I was scared of Mitch. When I faced Mitch during the series, he threw me a fastball, and I hit it 440 feet over the center field fence for a home run. After the game, the writer commended me on the home run, and I joked, "Yeah, but I was scared doing it." Who am I?

4. I had a laundry list of accomplishments. To name a few, I hit a grand slam in my first big league game in 1968, scored 110 or more runs five straight years (1969–73), and hit 25 or more home runs in a season for five different teams, including the Yankees, Angels, and Indians. Believe it or not, I lost my stroke so badly late in my career that I was sent back to the minors. My son has shown no signs of losing his stroke, though—in 1996, he hit his 333rd career home run to pass me, and in 1999, he moved up to 22nd on the all-time home run list, finishing the year with 445. Who am I?

5. If an eye injury hadn't forced me to retire prematurely after the 1995 season at the age of 34, I might have joined Lou Brock, Roberto Clemente, and the rest in the 3000-hit club. In just 12 seasons, I piled up 2304 hits, an average of 192 per year. I led my league in that category four times, with a high of 234 in 1988. Ten consecutive 80-RBI seasons, six Gold Gloves, and two World Series rings are more reasons why Cooperstown may await me. Mitch had these complimentary words about my attitude: "He was a fun guy to play against because he was always laughing and smiling, no matter what happened. You could throw a ball at his head and he'd just look out and laugh at you and then hit the next ball 900 feet." Well, maybe 450 feet. Who am I?

6. I'm a rarity in a lot of ways: I'm a shortstop with a slew of .300 seasons, who at least through 1999 has played my entire career for the same team in the same city in which I was born and went to high school. I'll give you some of my career highlights, and you ought to be able to come up with my name. In 1990, I helped my team win the World Series. In 1991, I tied a major league record by hitting five home runs in two games. In 1995, I won the National League MVP. In 1996, I became the first shortstop to hit 30 home runs and steal 30 bases in a season. (Alex Rodriguez became the second, in 1998.) For the life of me, though, I can't seem to hit a grand slam. In more than 6200 at bats, I still haven't parked one with the bases loaded. Who am I?

7. To win a Rookie of the Year Award, a Cy Young Award, an ERA title, two strikeout titles, fan 16 in a game three times, and pitch on a World Series winner in a career is pretty good—I did all that before I turned 22. Too much success so quickly was kind of hard to handle, and caused me some off-the-field problems and cost me some wins for a few years. Things hit rock bottom in the mid-1990s when I missed most of two seasons, but I got back on track in 1996 when I won 11 games and no-hit Lou Piniella's Mariners. Who am I?

8. I have a unique distinction: I'm the only pitcher who has won a Cy Young Award and guest-starred on *The Brady Bunch*. I won the Cy Young in 1962 when I led major league pitchers with 25 wins and 232 strikeouts. In 1965, I won 23, two less than my teammate Sandy Koufax. In 1968, I set a record—since broken by Orel Hershiser—when I pitched 58⅔ consecutive scoreless innings. And then in 1970, a year after I retired, I gave 15-year-old Greg Brady some tips on pitching. A lot of good it did him—he got a big head and his next game went out and was rocked for 12 runs in the first inning before the manager came out and gave him the hook. Who am I?

9. A lot of fans think I'm cocky and a showboat for my antics on the field, but Mitch tried to set them straight when he said I'm a nice, down-to-earth, unpretentious guy whose attitude is, "People are paying good money. I'm going to give them a show." Mitch said he played with guys who were cockier than I am who had less talent. I'm so unpretentious that one year while some of my teammates drove to games in their fancy cars, I rode my bicycle. Here are a few tidbits about my career: I was originally drafted by the Royals, but first played for the Yankees. I led the National League in triples with 14 in 1992. I stole 56 bases for the Reds in 1997 to finish second to Tony Womack. Finally—and I don't mean to sound cocky—I'm the only man who has played in both a World Series and a Super Bowl. Who am I?

10. I had a typical, ordinary, run-of-the-mill first major league at bat: I hit a home run off Nolan Ryan. It was a harbinger of things to come, as I hit 35 out of the park in my second year and have averaged almost 19 per season in my 14-year career (1986–99). My bat was never hotter than it was in the 1989 National League Championship Series when I hit .650, scored eight runs, and drove in eight to lead my team to a five-game win over Mitch's Cubs. Although I'm not much of a base stealer (I've yet to steal more than 12 in a season), over my career I've been difficult to double up. And I have a sense of humor, too. Early in my career, if somebody called my house and I wasn't there, my answering machine kicked on and the caller would hear the B.B. King song "The Thrill Is Gone," playing in the background. Who am I?

11. Every time I turned around in 1973, some pro sports team was drafting me. The Padres selected me in the first round of the baseball draft (I was first-team All-American my senior year as a pitcher/outfielder for the University of Minnesota), the NBA's Atlanta Hawks and ABA's Utah Jazz chose me in the fifth and sixth rounds, respectively, and even though I didn't play football in college, the Minnesota Vikings picked me in the 17th round of the NFL draft. In between signing with the Padres in 1973 and stroking my 3000th hit for the Twins in 1993, I hit 25 or more home runs nine times, drove in 100 runs eight times, and feuded with George Steinbrenner almost as much as Reggie and Billy. Who am I?

12. All these free agents who have been snapping up millions over the last 25 years owe me thank you notes. I had been a St. Louis Cardinals outfielder for 12 seasons—I hit .300 or more six of those years—and was quite displeased when the Redbirds traded me to the Phillies after the 1969 season in a six-player deal involving Dick Allen (he was called Richie then). I didn't feel like leaving St. Louis, so I refused to report to Philadelphia and started a big stink by filing suit in federal court, challenging baseball's reserve clause which bound a player forever to the team who held his contract. The court threw out my suit, but I stuck to my guns and, on principle, sat out the 1970 season. The Senators acquired my services, but I was ineffective, as I hit only .200 with two RBIs in 35 at bats in 1971. After I retired, though, the union kept fighting for free agency and eventually won. Who am I?

13. You don't have to be Peter Gammons to know that Tony Gwynn was the preeminent average hitter of the 1990s. Mr. Padre hit .344 over the decade and won four straight batting titles (1994–97) with marks of .394, .368, .353, and .372. I guess I beat out Tony for top honors in the 1980s: He also won four batting titles that decade with a high of .370 in 1987, but I won five, including four in a row from 1985 to 1988. I hit .352 in the 1980s and had a record seven straight 200-hit seasons, while Gwynn "only" hit .332. I didn't win any batting titles in the 1990s, but I hit .332 in 1991, .342 in 1994, and like Tony, collected my 3000th hit in 1999. All those hits and batting titles were nice, but nothing beat the feeling I had riding around Yankee Stadium on a horse after we beat the Braves to win the 1996 World Series. Who am I?

14. 1982 was a pretty good year for me: I was voted one of the 10 best casually dressed men in America, and my Cardinals team won the World Series. Other notables on the best dressed list included Alexander Haig and Johnny Carson. As a matter of fact, Johnny hosted *The Tonight Show* in Burbank, not far from where I grew up and went to Locke High School in Los Angeles. By coincidence, Lonnie Smith, one of the guys I played ball with as a teenager in L.A., was a teammate on my 1982 team. Lonnie had a long career in the majors—17 years—but I played 19 years. I only hit 28 home runs in those 19 seasons, and my lifetime average was less than .270, but my friends tell me I'll probably be voted into the Hall of Fame; I'll be up for induction in 2002. Who am I?

15. Mitch, who played with me part of one year, hit the nail on the head when he described me as a "blue-collar ballplayer": I just go out day after day and play hard, avoid controversy, and let my numbers do my talking for me. In 1991, I won the National League Rookie of the Year Award; my team had picked me up from the Red Sox minor league system the previous summer. I kept getting better every year, reaching the pinnacle in the strike-shortened 1994 season when I won the MVP unanimously by hitting .368 with 39 home runs, 116 RBIs, and a .750 slugging percentage, which was just a shade less than McGwire's .752 mark in 1998. I've kept trucking since, averaging 30 plus home runs and 110 RBIs per season, stealing a few bases, and playing a good first base. Who am I?

16. You know you've had a good career when you finish with more RBIs than Willie McCovey, Willie Stargell, and Mickey Mantle. I drove in 1652 runs, which is good for 18th on the all-time list and fourth among players who started their careers after 1960. I was in my prime from the late 1960s to the late 1970s when I knocked home 90 or more runs 11 straight years. I was proud to see my son Eduardo make it to the majors in 1993 with the Angels. In 1996, they traded him to the Reds, the team for which I picked up almost 1200 of those RBIs. Who am I?

17. Tony Gwynn may have waited 14 years between trips to the World Series, but I waited 16. I pitched in the 1979 Series for the Orioles against the Pirates, and did not appear in the Fall Classic again until 1995 for the Indians. (My 1983 Orioles team made it to the Series, but I didn't pitch.) That 1983 season was the beginning of a three-year struggle for me, both on and off the field. But then, after straightening out my personal problems, getting traded to the National League, and spending some time in the minors, I was resurrected. I had seven straight good years in the National League, especially 1991 when I led the loop in ERA, complete games, and shutouts. It looked like my days as a pitcher were over when the Mariners cut me loose in May 1997 after nine rocky starts, but I resurfaced in 1998 back in the National League at the ripe old age of 43 to pitch respectably as a middle reliever and spot starter. Who am I?

18. Major league scouts weren't exactly beating a path to my door when I was playing high school ball for Phoenixville High, outside Philadelphia—I was picked in the *62nd* round (the 1389th player) of the 1988 draft. I hung in there, though, made it to the majors, and after the 1998 season I signed a long-term contract for mega-millions. What did I do to justify that mammoth contract? I averaged .335, 33 home runs, and 106 RBIs a year over the previous six seasons, playing a position where guys usually hit .260 with half that many homers and runs batted in. I owe a lot to my godfather, who turned out to be my manager for the first four years of my major league career. Who am I?

19. If you walked by me on the street, you'd probably figure I was banging the boards in the NBA or laying some hits on an NFL quarterback, not playing on the more tranquil environs of the baseball diamond. I stood six-foot-six and at times, especially late in my career, tipped the scales at 265 pounds. I looked pretty intimidating to those hitters on the mound with my glare and hard heater. I led my league in saves four times, for the Cubs in 1983, Cardinals in 1991 and 1992, and Orioles in 1994. When I hung up my spikes in 1997 after a short stint with the Expos, I ranked number one on the all-time saves list with 478. I had a little fun in 1999 when Mitch and I teamed up for a commercial you may have seen. Mitch and I were playing some darts, and he kind of let one slip away, and it ended up puncturing the can I was drinking out of. "That," Mitch pointed out, "is why you should drink out of bottles." Who am I?

20. I get less respect than Rodney Dangerfield. I retired in 1992 with an impressive arsenal of stats. I'm third on the all-time strikeout list with 3701, behind only the Ryan Express and Super Steve Carlton. I won 287 games, which is more than a few guys whose plaques are on the wall in Cooperstown. I'm ninth on the career shutout list with 60. I had seven straight seasons in the 1970s with an ERA of 3.00 or less; one of those years, I threw a no-hitter. I pitched for two World Champions, the 1979 Pirates and 1987 Twins. What more do you want? But in the Hall of Fame votes since I became eligible for induction in 1998, only a small percentage of writers have been checking my name. Who am I?

Mixed Bag

21. In 1999, Mark McGwire became the 16th player to join baseball's coveted 500-home run club; he has slugged his home runs for two teams, the A's and the Cardinals. The other 15 club members are retired. Frank Robinson and Eddie Murray were the most traveled of the group as they both played for five different teams. Reggie Jackson and Jimmie Foxx played for four teams, while six other sluggers suited up for two or three teams. The five remaining players spent their entire careers with the same team. Who are they?

22. In their glory year of 1993, the Phillies won 97 games in the regular season, four against the Braves in the League Championship Series, and two against the Blue Jays in the World Series. How many of those 103 wins did Mitch save? It may help to know that this number is also the regular season home run high for Joe DiMaggio (1937), Orlando Cepeda (1961), and Jim Rice (1978). Kudos if you get it right on the nose; feel free to take half-credit if you're within two.

23. Of course you remember the Marlins won the 1997 World Series in just their fifth year in existence, and the Cubbies haven't been to the Fall Classic since 1945, but can you remember how these teams fared in the Series over the last two decades?

Cleveland Indians	**A.** Lost two Series in the 1990s
Minnesota Twins	**B.** Won a Series in the 1990s
San Diego Padres	**C.** Won a Series in the 1980s
New York Mets	**D.** Lost a Series in the 1980s and the 1990s
Cincinnati Reds	**E.** Won a Series in the 1980s and the 1990s

24. In baseball's storied history, players have acquired some unforgettable nicknames such as "The Georgia Peach" (Ty Cobb), "The Chairman of the Board" (Whitey Ford), and "The Say Hey Kid" (Willie Mays). Other players, whether they liked it or not, were nicknamed after members of the animal kingdom. We'll give you the nicknames and some quick clues about a few of these players, and you tell us who they are.

A. "The Penguin" held down the starting third-base job for two National League teams in the 1970s and 1980s and played in six All-Star Games.

B. "The Cobra" won National League batting titles in 1977 and 1978 for the Pirates and finished with more than 2700 hits.

C. It was a pleasure to watch "The Bird" talk to baseballs and flap his arms on the mound when he won 19 games for the Tigers his rookie season in 1976.

D. "The Hawk" graciously patrolled the outfield for 21 years, winning eight Gold Gloves, and also hitting 438 home runs.

E. "Bulldog" was a fixture in Tommy Lasorda's starting rotation for 10 years; in 1999 he won his 200th career game for a team on the East Coast.

25. Some time in the 21st century, a player may break Hank Aaron's home run record, Pete Rose's hit record, and Joe DiMaggio's record for longest hitting streak, but as Phillies broadcaster Richie Ashburn used to say, "you can bet the house" that nobody will break Cal Ripken Jr's record for consecutive games played, which ended on September 20, 1998, at an astonishing 2632. Ripken's streak got so much hype, you may have forgotten that over in the National League, there have been two players since 1960 who put together streaks of more than 1000 straight games. From 1963 to 1970, an outfielder played in 1117 consecutive games. He held the National League record until 1983, when a first baseman who hadn't missed a game since 1975 played in number 1118 in a row. An injury ended his streak later that year at 1207. Their final career statistics were strikingly similar. The outfielder finished with 2711 hits, 434 doubles, 1475 RBIs, 90 stolen bases, and a .290 batting average. The first baseman ended up with 2599 hits, 440 doubles, 1308 RBIs, 83 stolen bases, and a .294 batting average. Name these iron men.

26. If you think a player has to be a star to win an MVP, you're mistaken. While the great ones have won their share of MVPs, once in a while a player who is not considered a star, such as Jeff Burroughs (1974 A.L.), Willie Hernandez (1984 A.L.), and Kevin Mitchell (1989 N.L.), has an amazing season and wins the award. On the other hand, the MVP has eluded some players who put together outstanding careers. Which one of these fine players never won the prestigious MVP Award?
  A. Eddie Murray
  B. Orlando Cepeda
  C. Robin Yount
  D. Jim Rice
  E. Willie McCovey

27. You hear so much about MVP, Cy Young, and Rookie of the Year awards that Gold Glove awards, which are given every year to the best fielders at each position in both leagues, sometimes get overlooked. Ask any manager, though, and he'll tell you until you're blue in the face about how a Gold Glover shores up his defense. With a little help, you should be able to name the players at each position with the most Gold Gloves. We'll give you each player's position, the team for which he has played the most games in his career, his total seasons, and the number of Gold Gloves he has won. (One is active, so his numbers are through 1999.)

Position	Team	Total Seasons	Gold Gloves
Pitcher	Twins	25	16
Catcher	Reds	17	10
First base	Cardinals	17	11
Second base	Cubs	16	9
Shortstop	Cardinals	19	13
Third base	Orioles	23	16
Outfield	Pirates	18	12
Outfield	Giants	22	12
Outfield	Tigers	22	10
Outfield	Mariners	11	10

28. We couldn't have written a baseball quiz book without including one question on "The Bambino" himself, George Herman "Babe" Ruth. You have to admire a guy who, when asked in the midst of the Depression whether he thought it was all right for him to get paid a higher annual salary than President Herbert Hoover, responded, "Why not? I had a better year than he did." Here are 10 statements about the Babe. We want to know if they're true or false.

A. He stole more than 100 bases in his career.
B. He finished his career with the Boston Braves.
C. He was born in New York and died in Baltimore.
D. He was a 20-game winner for the Red Sox.
E. His career average was higher than teammate Lou Gehrig's.
F. He is the all-time career leader in RBIs.
G. He holds the American League record for most strikeouts in a season by a batter.
H. He was six feet, two inches tall.
I. He hit .400 in a season once.
J. He didn't drink, smoke, or carouse.

29. Mitch isn't the first baseball player to write a book. Quite a few books have been penned by or about baseball players ranging from controversial (*Ball Four*) to poignant (*You Could've Made Us Proud*) to funny (*Some of My Best Friends Are Crazy*). Match these players with the books they authored or co-authored.

Jay Johnstone	**A.** *Me & the Spitter*
Sparky Lyle	**B.** *The Bronx Zoo*
Jim Bouton	**C.** *Some of My Best Friends Are Crazy*
Gaylord Perry	**D.** *Ball Four*
Joe Pepitone	**E.** *You Could've Made Us Proud*

30. When chronic back problems finally convinced popular Yankees first baseman Don Mattingly to call it quits after the 1995 season, he retired having played his entire career with the same team. Among guys who played in the majors for at least 10 years that's not common, especially in recent years. Here are five other players who never changed uniforms. We're pretty generous here, giving you each player's team, years played, and a sentence or two about his career. You should rattle off the first three in no time; you may have to think about the last two unless you're an Orioles or Royals fan.

Team	Years Played	Career Highlights
Tigers	1977–95	Held down the Tigers second base job for virtually his entire career. Finished with 2369 hits, four more than his longtime double play partner.
Yankees	1975–88	"Louisiana Lightnin'" was at the top of his game in 1978 when he was 25-3 with a 1.74 ERA.
Reds	1970–88	Overshadowed by Bench, Perez, Morgan, and Rose, this player was a frequent All-Star selection.
Orioles	1976–88	Crafty lefty with great control; 1.63 ERA in post-season.
Royals	1970–84	Quietly won 166 games with a high of 20 in 1973.

31. The catcher practically didn't have to use signs when Mitch was pitching—he almost always threw his heater. Some pitchers aren't able to get by on just their fastballs; they need a unique pitch to help get hitters out. Match these stellar relievers of yesteryear with the specialty pitches that they threw.

Bruce Sutter	**A.** Knuckleball
Tug McGraw	**B.** Forkball
Hoyt Wilhelm	**C.** Screwball
Dave Giusti	**D.** Split-fingered fastball
Elroy Face	**E.** Palmball

32. From the late 1940s until the early 1980s, there were three sure things in life: death, taxes, and this colorful character going to the World Series. Over a 35-year period (1947–81), he suited up for 21 Fall Classics: 14 as a player, five as a coach, and two as a manager, and his team came out on the long end of the stick 13 times. One final hint, which should clinch it for you. The story has it that one time he went to pick up a pizza for one and was asked whether he wanted it cut in four or eight slices. "You better make it four," he said, "I could never eat eight."

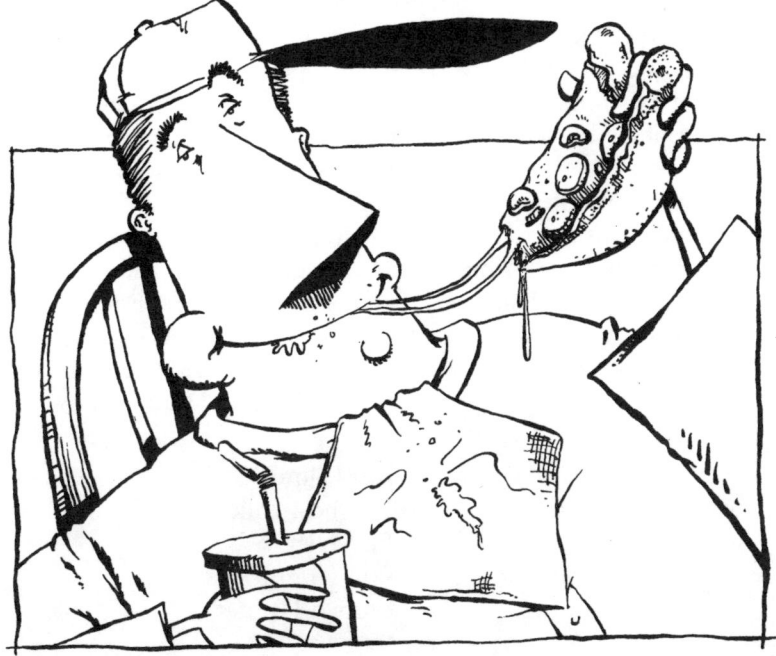

33. All right, quick now, name the only two players who started their careers in 1975 or later who collected at least 3250 hits. We'll add that they combined for 738 home runs and 614 stolen bases.

34. If you don't know which National League team won the most regular-season games in the 1990s, you've been watching too much football. Figuring out which American League team won the most games in the decade will require more thought. Have the Yankees' strong seasons with Joe Torre at the helm been enough to make up for the years in the early '90s when they struggled? How about the Indians, who also came on strong in the mid-'90s? Or could it be the steady Red Sox? What about the 1960s? The Dodgers won the World Series in 1963 and 1965, but did they win more games during the decade than the Cardinals? Looking back over the last five decades, tell us which team in each league won the most regular-season games.

35. Every January, as fans count the days until the start of spring training, baseball writers across America cast their ballots for the players whom they believe are worthy of induction into the Hall of Fame. A player is eligible for induction the first January after he's been retired five years and must be named on 75 percent of ballots. If a player fails to receive five percent of votes in a year, his name is removed from the ballot. If a player does not get elected after 15 years, his name is removed from the baseball writers' ballots, but he becomes eligible for induction by the Veterans Committee. It goes without saying that a player must be tremendous in order to be inducted into the hallowed halls of Cooperstown, but normally only the superstars of superstars are elected on the first ballot. For each of the 10 players listed below, indicate an A if he was elected the first year he was eligible, B if he made it from the second year to the fifth year, C if he was elected on ballot numbers six through 10, and D if he was voted in by the Veterans Committe.

Willie Stargell	Jim Palmer
Luis Aparicio	Harmon Killebrew
Roy Campanella	Phil Niekro
Reggie Jackson	Phil Rizzuto
Jim Bunning	Catfish Hunter

36. Here's one for you hoop fans. A handful of guys have been gifted enough athletes to play major league baseball and pro basketball. One basketball player of some repute also played minor league baseball for one year to break up the monotony of winning NBA scoring titles and championships. For basketball enthusiasts, these will be layups for you, but if you've been too busy over the years tuning in to baseball to keep up on basketball, these will be jumpers from the baseline.

  A. Why hit .220 as a part-time infielder and finish in last place for the Blue Jays when you can help Larry Bird and Robert Parish win NBA titles for the Celtics? That's what this Brigham Young product said.
  B. He pitched well for the White Sox in 1962 and 1963, as he posted a 2.90 ERA in 102 innings. But he decided basketball was his game—and he was right. He starred for the Knicks for 10 years.
  C. He started as a forward with the Detroit Pistons, then switched to baseball and pitched 20 years, mostly for the Braves and Phillies.
  D. This current major league skipper managed Michael Jordan when he took his hiatus from the NBA to play minor league ball for the Southern League's Birmingham Barons in 1994.

37. The Yankees closed out the century in a grand fashion. In 1998, they set an American League record with 114 regular-season wins and then swept the Rangers in the Division Series, beat the Indians four games to two in the League Championship Series, and swept the Padres in the World Series. Their two losses in the post-season was the fewest since the three-tier post-season system was first used in 1995. In 1999, the Yankees were less of a juggernaut during the season as they won 98 games, but they were even more dominating in the post-season. They again swept the Rangers in the Division Series, beat the Red Sox four games to one in the League Championship Series, and whitewashed the Braves in the World Series; thus, the 1999 Yankees lost only one game in the post-season. From 1969 to 1993, when baseball utilized two post-season rounds (there were three rounds in the strike-shortened 1981 season), only one team went undefeated by sweeping both the League Championship Series and the World Series. Who was it?

38. The baseball gods must not have wanted him to manage in a World Series. In 1964, his Phillies led the National League by six and a half games with two weeks left. So sure that the Phils would hang on and win the pennant, the team printed World Series tickets. But they dropped 10 in a row, allowing the Cardinals to overtake them for the flag. In 1982, he piloted the Angels to the American League Western Division Championship, won the first two games of the best-of-five playoff series against the Brewers only to drop the last three games. Lightning struck again in 1986 when he came within not only a game of the World Series, but an out. The League Championship Series had been extended to seven games, and his Angels led the Red Sox three games to one and took a 5–2 lead into the ninth inning of the fifth game. The Sox scored four to take the lead, eventually won the game in 11 innings, then returned to Boston to thump his demoralized squad 10–4 and 8–1. He also managed the Expos for seven years and the Twins for five, but never finished higher than third for either. Name this hard-luck skipper.

39. In case you've never been there, Donora is a small town about 15 miles south of Pittsburgh. Its population of approximately 6000 is less than one-thousandth the population of New York City, yet it is the birthplace of three major leaguers with a combined 7500 hits and 1000 home runs. The oldest of the three closed out his 22-year career in 1963 with 3630 hits and 475 home runs. Ten years after he retired, another Donora native cracked the big leagues and remained there for 19 years. His final numbers: 2143 hits and 152 home runs. The youngest of the group is active and his hands are the quickest Mitch has ever seen. If he stays healthy, he might bring down Aaron's home run record. Name this trio of Donorians.

40. Mitch wore number 99 in the Phillies' 1993 season and also for the Astros and Angels after his childhood hero, NFL star defensive end Mark Gastineau. The Phillies aren't going to retire Mitch's 99; after all, they've only retired the numbers of four players in their history: Hall-of-Famers Richie Ashburn (1), Mike Schmidt (20), Steve Carlton (32), and Robin Roberts (36). The Yankees, on the other hand, have retired 15 players' numbers. Here are five questions on retired numbers—not only are these hanging curveballs, they're belt high right across the middle of the plate.

   A. Two American League teams retired this Panamanian's number 29. For the first team, he hit .334; for the second, he hit .314.
   B. After this right-hander (who threw two-hitters) died of carbon monoxide poisoning in 1975 at the age of 29, the Astros retired his number 40.
   C. Pirates brass decided that no player should have the privilege of wearing this great's number 21 after his death in 1972.
   D. "The Old Professor" had the honor of having his number 37 retired by two teams, the Yankees and the Mets.
   E. Thirteen 20-win seasons and 363 career wins made this player a shoo-in to have his number 21 retired by the Braves.

41. Mitch, his Phillies teammate Lenny Dykstra, and Dave Stieb, the Blue Jays all-time winningest pitcher, were all born in this town:
   A. Lubbock, Texas
   B. Springfield, New Jersey
   C. Santa Ana, California
   D. South Bend, Indiana
   E. Tampa, Florida

42. Some of baseball's best managers in recent years did not have stellar careers as major league players. Tony LaRussa hit .199 in 176 at bats with no home runs, Tommy Lasorda was 0–4 with an ERA of 6.52, and Jim Leyland never played a game in the big leagues. Many managers, however, had formidable careers. Try to match these skippers, who were piloting teams in 1999, with their career home run totals:

Art Howe	**A.** 136
Joe Torre	**B.** 252
Felipe Alou	**C.** 206
Phil Garner	**D.** 109
Davey Johnson	**E.** 43

43. Somebody should sue the Yankees for unfairly monopolizing winning the World Series. In 1999, the Yanks won the Series for the 25th time, more than a quarter of all World Series. Two teams rank second with a very distant nine World Championships. Some teams have only won it all once or twice since the Series was first played in 1903. Match these five teams with the number of World Series that they have won.

Chicago Cubs	**A.** 9
St. Louis Cardinals	**B.** 6
Brooklyn/Los Angeles Dodgers	**C.** 4
Philadelphia Phillies	**D.** 2
Detroit Tigers	**E.** 1

44. These players all have several things in common: They hit between 200 and 300 career home runs, played for four or more teams, and retired in the 1980s. For each player, we're going to give you the years he played, number of home runs he hit, and the teams for whom he played, in order. Your mission is to identify the players. Three correct will impress us.

	Years	Home Runs	Teams
A.	1971–88	267	A's, Indians, Padres, Cardinals, Pirates, Angels
B.	1972–87	234	Giants, Braves, Phillies, Cubs, Mariners
C.	1976–89	251	Pirates, A's, Red Sox, Angels
D.	1971–83	207	Pirates, White Sox, Rangers, Mariners
E.	1969–83	201	A's, Padres, Cardinals, Pirates

45. Since you're in the groove of remembering players who retired in the 1980s, here are five well-traveled pitchers who won between 200 and 300 games and who called it quits in the '80s. (One actually pitched eight innings in 1990.) Same deal—for each player, we'll give you the years he pitched in the majors, total wins, and teams for whom he pitched, again in order. Because 200 wins is more of an accomplishment than 200 home runs, and therefore these pitchers are slightly more well-known than the hitters in the previous question, you'll need four out of five to earn our respect.

	Years	Wins	Teams
A.	1965–83	284	Phillies, Cubs, Rangers, Red Sox, Rangers, Cubs
B.	1963–89	288	Indians, White Sox, Dodgers, Yankees, Angels, A's, Yankees
C.	1967–85	222	Mets, Twins, White Sox, Phillies
D.	1967–88	221	Cubs, Padres, Tigers, Braves, Astros, Yankees, Twins
E.	1969–90	220	Cardinals, Astros, Pirates, Dodgers, Reds, Angels, White Sox, Brewers, Pirates

46. Isn't it about time some player won the Triple Crown? After all, it's been more than 30 years—since 1967—when a player led his league with a .326 average, 44 home runs, and 121 RBIs. These were the only home run and RBI titles this player won in his long and accomplished career, but he also won batting titles in 1963 and 1968. He's second to Pete Rose on the all-time games played list with 3308, seventh in career hits with 3419, and 11th in lifetime RBIs with 1844. Can you name him?

47. This one goes out to all you guys and gals whose enthusiasm has been dampened by Astroturf, free agency, and the designated hitter rule, and who enjoy reminiscing about the glorious decade of the 1950s when three guys named Mickey, Duke, and Willie were playing center field in New York.
- **A.** "The Giants win the pennant! The Giants win the pennant!" exclaimed New York Giants broadcaster Russ Hodges when this player connected for a three-run homer in the bottom of the ninth inning of the third and deciding game of the 1951 playoff series against the Dodgers, to give the Giants a 5–4 win and a trip to the World Series.
- **B.** In 1954, the Indians posted a staggering 111–43 record for a .721 percentage, higher than the 1998 Yankees. Anchoring the pitching staff were two future Hall-of-Famers, who each won 23 games that year.
- **C.** He was 3–21 in 1954 and 1–10 in 1960, but in Game 5 of the 1956 World Series for the Yankees, he set down 27 straight Dodgers for the only perfect game—in fact, the only no-hitter—in Series history.

D. This right-hander brought Milwaukee its only World Championship in 1957 by winning three games in the Series against the Yankees, including shutouts in Games 5 and 7.

48. Name the team: They have only been to one World Series since 1919 and they lost. Luke Appling is their all-time hit leader. Ted Lyons is their all-time wins leader. Nellie Fox won the MVP for them in 1959. Tommie Agee won the Rookie of the Year for them in 1966. Jeff Torborg and Jim Fregosi have managed the team. If we told you much more, we'd give it away.

49. Name the city: Casey Stengel managed there for six years in the late 1930s and 1940s and didn't finish higher than fifth place. Eddie Mathews started his major league career there in 1952. Jim Lonborg won a Cy Young Award for this city's team in 1967. John McNamara managed the team in this city to the World Series in the 1980s. Rick Aguilera pitched a half-season there in 1995 and led the club in saves.

50. Since the Giants moved west to San Francisco prior to the 1958 season, six of their players have won RBI titles. Would you believe that Willie Mays, who ranks eighth on the all-time list with 1907 ribbies, is not one of the six? Willie didn't win one the seven years he played for the Giants in New York either. Two of the six San Francisco Giants who won RBI titles did so in the 1960s, two in the 1980s, and two in the 1990s. We're talking about some excellent hitters here, so we don't see why you can't get at least four or five of these guys, and maybe all six.

CHANGE-UPS AT THE LETTERS

Who Am I?

51. To give you an idea how slow I am, in the decade of the 1990s, I amassed almost 4200 at bats and hit the grand total of five triples and stole a mere four bases. Incidentally, in about the same number of at bats during the '90s, Cecil Fielder's numbers in those categories were five and two respectively. But as Cecil well knows, it doesn't much matter if you can't run as long as you can hit. I'm a career .292 hitter, and in 1999, I reached the 20–home run mark for the eleventh time. One of my former teams thought so much of me, they had a special day for me in 1990 at which they retired my number. My speech wasn't exactly a filibuster—I spoke just 16 words. Who am I?

52. In a game brimming with big, bruising first basemen like Mark McGwire and Tony Clark who strike out often and hit a lot of home runs, I've been an anomaly: I don't hit many home runs, and I don't strike out much. McGwire practically hit more home runs in 1998 and 1999 (135) than I've hit in my entire 12-year career (137). The 17 and 16 that I hit in 1998 and 1999 are my career highs. (I also hit 16 in 1995.) But I'm not a perennial 100-strikeout guy like those behemoths. I've never fanned even *60* times in a season, and in 1993, I struck out only 32 times in 594 at bats. I have a much more compact stroke than Clark and company, which cuts down on the K's and also results in a ton of line drives. I've finished in the top 10 in hitting eight times and have hit less than .295 in a season just once. I also racked up more hits than any major leaguer in the 1990s (1754). And by the way, Mitch and I were teammates for two years, and we used to kill time during rain delays playing cards in the clubhouse. Who am I?

53. Appearances can be deceiving: I looked like I should be flipping burgers in some greasy spoon—or so Mitch thought—not spraying line drives all over major league parks, which I did for a decade. I was a .300 hitter in seven of my 10 seasons, and I hit 20 or more home runs twice—for the 1987 Padres and 1991 Phillies. I also played first base with agility, despite my roly-poly build. After I wrapped up things with the White Sox in 1995 (I finished with some round numbers: 1200 games, 100 home runs, and a .300 average), I made my way back to West Virginia where for a while I ran a bar that I called "The Third Base," because it's the last place you would stop before going home. Who am I?

54. Year in and year out, I've been one of the game's steadiest power hitters since my rookie year with the Blue Jays in 1987. I've hit 25 or more homers in a season 10 times, and driven in 90 or more runs in a season nine times. Big Mac and I are the only players who have won home run titles in both leagues. In 1991, I became one of a handful of players in history to hit grand slams in consecutive games when I accomplished the feat for the Padres. My 10 post-season home runs rank high among active players. One of my most prodigious home runs came in 1988 against the Rangers when I was with the Blue Jays. Mitch remembers it better than I do. It came off a rookie right-hander named Scott May, who would never win a major league game. Before the game, May was bragging to the Rangers pitchers about his 97-mile-per-hour fastball. I quickly put him in his place when I belted a home run off him that went about 500 feet. Mitch and the other relievers were joking in the bullpen, "That May sure has a great 97-mile-per-hour fastball." Who am I?

55. If Reggie Jackson was "Mr. October," I guess I was "Mr. April." Over a period of a few years, I rattled off 20 straight wins in April before the streak was snapped in 1991. I was no slouch in October, either—I was 8–0 in American League Championship Series play and won two World Series games. In between April and October, I earned my money, too. I was a 20-game winner four consecutive years (1987–90)—I'm the only pitcher to do that since Jim Palmer won 20 games in four straight years for the Orioles in the 1970s. What else can I tell you about myself? I pitched a no-hitter in 1990 against the Blue Jays (for whom I later pitched) on the same day that my former Dodgers teammate Fernando Valenzuela was no-hitting the Cardinals. Who am I?

56. In 1999, for the first time since 1985, I failed to lead my team in saves. Pitching for two clubs, I paced my staff in saves a record 13 straight years, from 1986 to 1998. (I was tied for the team lead in 1992.) I led my league in three of those seasons (1988, 1990, and 1994), and my career ERA through 1999 is just 2.64. I've pitched in more than 875 games, and every one has been as a reliever. Despite all my saves, I didn't pitch in the post-season until 1999, although before that year my team had finished second in the division six times. Who am I?

57. Mitch will be the first one to tell you that in my prime, I had ungodly power. When I was with the Blue Jays, I hit a grand slam off him at Toronto's old Exhibition Stadium that just missed hitting the roof in left field. As Mitch pointed out, "For anybody who has been there, that's a huge home run." I had some fairly huge years for the Blue Jays, but nothing like 1987 when I hit 47 home runs with a league-leading 134 RBIs en route to winning the MVP. I slowed down a little after my MVP year, and when the Blue Jays wanted to move me out of left field and make me a designated hitter, I opted to sign as a free agent with the Cubs. I played one year on the north side of Chicago, finishing with respectable home run and RBI figures of 25 and 86, but then right before the start of the regular season in 1992, the Cubs traded me cross-town to the White Sox for relief pitcher Ken Patterson and another player (born in the same province in the Dominican Republic as I was), a 23-year-old wiry outfielder with awesome bat speed named Sammy Sosa. Who am I?

58. I don't like to brag, but I'm the fastest person Mitch has ever seen. Funny thing is, I wasn't that much of a base stealer. Twenty-seven was my high in a season, and I swiped just one base in my final 183 games. Power was my forte—I hit 107 homers for the Royals from 1987 to 1990, and added one in the 1989 All-Star Game. Unfortunately, I struck out way too often; I averaged 151 K's a season during that four-year period. A hip injury cut short my baseball career—and my football career, for that matter. Who am I?

59. I spent my winters collecting stamps and my summers collecting walks and home runs. I walked 100 or more times in five seasons and ended my 21-year career with 1605 free passes to rank ninth on the all-time list. I racked up the walks mainly for two reasons: I had a good eye, and pitchers sometimes pitched around me because of my power—I hit 414 career home runs, which were split almost evenly among the three teams for which I played. I hit 131 for my first team, 142 for the second, and 141 for the third. I had 40 home run seasons for my first and third teams (in 1973 and 1985, respectively) and a 30–home run year for my second team (in 1983). The raps on me at times were that I didn't drive in enough runs (I only had one 100-RBI year) and I didn't hit for a high enough average (my lifetime mark was an ordinary .248). One final note of interest: In the late 1960s, I played college basketball at Pasadena City College, where my coach was none other than future UNLV coach Jerry Tarkanian. Who am I?

60. I provided some entertainment in the 1997 All-Star Game when I batted against Randy Johnson. I'm a left-handed hitter who wasn't used to facing six-foot-ten lefties who throw fastballs in the high 90s and sometimes have control problems. Randy and I had been teammates for the Expos briefly in the late 1980s, but I had never batted against him in a game. My first time up, he threw one high and tight, and I said to myself, "Wait a minute, I don't think I'm too crazy about getting drilled by 'The Big Unit.'" So, as a joke, I walked across the plate, turned my helmet around backwards, and assumed a right-handed stance. Randy threw me a ball, and I got my nerve back up, and went back to batting left-handed. I earned my trip to the All-Star Game that year because I batted .366, hit a league-leading 49 home runs, and drove in 130 runs. I also earned my selections to the Mid-Season Classic in 1998 and 1999 as I won the batting title both years with averages of .363 and .379 and also led the league in slugging in 1999, with a sizzling .710. Who am I?

61. My nickname should have been "Mr. Superstitious." If a box of bats came back with my name slightly off-center, sorry, I'd send them back. Sometimes, if I didn't get a hit my first at bat, I'd change my batting glove or uniform. After all, it couldn't have been *my* fault that I grounded out; it must have been the batting glove or uniform. Because of the way I hustled and dove, my uniform was always getting dirty anyway. When asked why my team's stadium was getting new dirt, our clubhouse manager cracked that all the old dirt was on my uniform. My superstitiousness and hustle must have paid off because I hit .300 three times, including 1990 when I finished second to Willie McGee for the National League batting championship. When I scored 143 runs in 1993, it was the most by a National League player in 61 years. And when October rolled around, it was show time for me: In 32 post-season games, I hit 10 home runs and slugged a stupendous .661. Who am I?

62. More than 20 players are in the "30–30" club (30 home runs and 30 stolen bases in a season), but I'm the only switch-hitter, and am also the only player in the "30–30–30" club (30 home runs, 30 stolen bases, *and* 30 errors in a season). I had the year in which I combined power, speed, and a shaky glove for the Mets in 1991 when I hit a league-leading 38 homers (and drove in a league-leading 117 runs), stole 30 bases, and made 31 errors, most of them at third base. I had two other "30–30" seasons for the Mets (1987 and 1989) without the 30 errors. I played most of my career with the Queens boys, but I started with the Tigers and finished up with the Rockies and Cubs. Who am I?

63. When I broke into the majors in 1979, I ran like a gazelle and hit tape-measure home runs, prompting people to compare me to Mickey Mantle. I was fast and had power, but trust me, I was no Mick. I had seasons in which I stole 34, 31, 30, 29, and 26 bases. In the home runs department, I never cracked the 30 barrier, but I had seasons of 29, 28, 27, 25, 24, and 23. The most dramatic home run of my career? I don't have to think long on that one. Game 1 of the 1988 World Series, bottom of the ninth inning, we were behind 4–3. I was unable to run because of hamstring and knee injuries, but hobbled to the plate as a pinch-hitter off Dennis Eckersely with two outs and a runner on second base. The count ran full, I fouled off a couple pitches, and then lined a two-run homer into the right field bleachers to win the game. I played a few more years until I decided to retire in the middle of the 1995 season. When asked why, I responded, "I've been traded to my family." Who am I?

64. Like Alex Rodriguez, Andruw Jones, and a few others, I was on the big league diamond as a teenager. I quickly established myself as a top defensive catcher with a howitzer of an arm. Consistently, I have thrown out about half the runners who've tried to steal on me, and have won the Gold Glove. Hitting didn't come quite as easily. It took me about three years to get the hang of major league pitching, but once I did, I haven't looked back. In 1999, I reached the top of my game, as I hit .332 with 35 home runs and 113 RBIs and edged out Pedro Martinez, Roberto Alomar, and Rafael Palmiero for the American League MVP. Who am I?

65. I hit .300 more often than Bill Buckner and Fred Lynn, and got haircuts less often than Mitch and John Kruk. I hit .300 seven times in my 21 seasons with a high of .332 in 1975. And I made it a point to avoid barber shops—for part of my career, my hair spilled out of my helmet onto my shoulders. When I was 13, about the time I thought wearing my hair long was cool, I started hitting from both sides of the plate and eventually became one of baseball's best switch-hitters. I finished with more career hits than Mickey Mantle, and I rank number one in hits among catchers, beating out receivers who could really swing the bat, like Carlton Fisk and Bill Dickey. I played in one World Series in my long career—for the 1982 Brewers—and I homered in the first two games against my former team, the Cardinals. Who am I?

66. I finished my career dead even: 216 wins and 216 losses. I won the majority of those games as a starter with the Rangers in the 1980s, after I had spent the 1970s toiling predominantly out of the Dodgers bullpen. By the time I hung up my spikes in 1994 with the Marlins, I was 46 years old and had pitched in the majors for 25 years. I think the keys to my longevity were that I threw mostly knuckleballs, and that I didn't tire myself out chasing fly balls during pre-game workouts. When I was with the Rangers, while the rest of the pitchers were working up a sweat running after fly balls, I couldn't be bothered: I would stand in the right field corner and throw balls up against the wall. One day in 1986, Mitch, who was 21, asked me why I never caught fly balls. "It's simple, youngster," I told him, "I'd rather look lazy than bad." Who am I?

67. I was a flame-thrower in my early years for the Angels. Pitching on the same staff with Nolan Ryan in 1975, I led the American League in strikeouts with 269; in 1976, I won 19 and fanned 261 to finish second in K's to Nolan; and in 1977, I led the league with a 2.54 ERA and struck out 17 batters in one game. I developed some arm problems at about that time, which shaved some velocity off my fastball; and the rest of my career, I was a dependable but unspectacular pitcher. After 1977, I never struck out more than 160 batters in a season, nor recorded an ERA less than 3.00. But I was a workhorse. I was in a team's starting rotation every year until I retired in 1993; several of those seasons were spent in the city in which I grew up and went to high school, Detroit. All told, I started 616 games to rank 14th on the all-time list and struck out 2773 batters to rank 15th on the list. I finished ahead of Bob Feller, Early Wynn, and Robin Roberts in both categories, and those fellows are all in the Hall. Despite my impressive numbers, I won't be joining them— I received nary a vote from the 497 writers who cast their ballots in 1999, my first year of eligibility. Never pitching in a World Series undoubtedly hurt my cause. Who am I?

68. I've been described as outspoken, controversial, and argumentative—especially by managers and sportswriters. In 1996, Davey Johnson, my manager for the Orioles, insisted on using me as a designated hitter instead of playing me in the field, which made no sense to me—I'd only led the league in errors at my position three times. I was later quoted as saying that I wouldn't let Johnson manage my rotisserie team. Before I went to Baltimore, I spent three and a half tumultuous years arguing with sportswriters and listening to those New York boo birds. Say what you want about my personality (by the way, Mitch, who played winter ball with me, will vouch for me that I'm a great guy), I've been a pretty productive player over the years, although I had a sub-par 1999 season. I've played in six All-Star Games, hold the National League record for most home runs by a switch-hitter, and helped the Marlins win it all in 1997. Who am I?

69. In his book *Whatever Happened to the Hall of Fame?*, Bill James hailed me as "one of the most underrated players in baseball history." According to Mitch, I'm also one of the strongest. One night in Texas, a brawl broke out over a disagreement between Mitch and my teammate Marty Barrett, and I played the role of peacemaker: I grabbed Mitch and held him so he couldn't get at Barrett. I used my strength to club almost 400 home runs and gun out runners consistently from right field in my 20-year career, nearly all of which was spent in the same American League city. My team made it to the World Series twice, once in the 1970s and once in the 1980s, and both times we lost in seven games. Who am I?

70. I hit one of the most memorable home runs in Cardinals history: a three-run shot off the Dodgers' Tom Niedenfuer in the top of the ninth inning of the sixth game of the 1985 League Championship Series to win the game 7–5 and the Series 4–2. Mitch later faced me when I was with the Yankees and Padres, and he considered me one of the two hitters that he least liked to pitch to. (The other was Dave Winfield.) By that stage of my career, not only was I banging out home runs, I had developed a great eye. I led my league in walks three times and averaged 116 walks a season over a five-year stretch (1987–1991). In one double-header in 1987, I took the trot down to first base six times. I was less patient at the plate when I came up to the majors in the mid-1970s. For example, in 1978 I only walked 50 times, but I hit .306—my best average for a full season—and compiled a 26-game hitting streak, which got virtually ignored because it occurred amid Pete Rose's National League record 44-game streak. Who am I?

Mixed Bag

71. Since the Baseball Writers Association of America began to select Most Valuable Players in 1931, excluding active players Barry Bonds (1992–93) and Frank Thomas (1993–94), nine players have won the prestigious award in back-to-back seasons. Coincidentally, the nine players fill out the positions on the diamond: one pitcher, one catcher, one first baseman, one second baseman, one shortstop, one third baseman, and three outfielders. Seven are in the Hall of Fame, one isn't in and probably won't get elected, and one, who retired in 1993 with 398 home runs, may make it. How many can you name?

72. Here are 10 managers, some of whom Mitch played for in the majors, and some of whom he did not. For each, tell us whether Mitch played for him, and if he did, tell us which team.

Bobby Valentine   Jim Riggleman
Don Zimmer   Johnny Oates
Jim Fregosi   Terry Collins
Kevin Kennedy   Buck Rodgers
Davey Johnson   Marcel Lachemann

73. These players all share the same last name: a Tigers outfielder from the 1960s and 1970s who collected 107 career pinch-hits; one of the starting outfielders for the Padres in their early years who was nicknamed "Downtown"; one of baseball's top pitchers today who signed a monstrous contract after the 1998 season; and a third baseman for the Giants in the mid-1980s who started out strong, but fizzled quickly. Who are they?

74. Let's try it again. Here are four more players with the same last name: the only player who was ever traded for Willie Mays; the Hall-of-Famer whose goal, legend has it, was to walk down the street and have people say, "There goes the greatest hitter who ever lived"; the switch-hitting Yankee who won the 1998 American League batting title; and a happy-go-lucky player nicknamed "No Neck" who shared the White Sox outfield a generation ago with the likes of Ken Berry, Carlos May, and Rick Reichardt. Who are the four?

75. It was one of the best trades the Tigers ever made in the short term and one of the worst they made in the long term. In the middle of a battle for the American League Eastern Division title with the Blue Jays, on August 12, 1987, Detroit acquired a 36-year-old pitcher with 17 years of major league experience from a National League team for a highly touted 20-year-old prospect who had not yet pitched in the majors. The veteran pickup was phenomenal down the stretch, posting a 9–0 record and 1.53 ERA to help Alan Trammell, Jack Morris, and the rest of the Tigers overcome the Blue Jays for the division. Even though they lost to the Twins in the League Championship Series, they wouldn't have gotten there if they hadn't made the key trade. It was the last hurrah for that pitcher, as his ERA shot back up to 4.32 the following season. In 1989, his last major league season, he won 6 and lost a league-leading 18 games. Meanwhile, the hot prospect whom the Tigers dealt developed into one of baseball's most highly regarded pitchers. He has won 14 or more games in a season seven times, including a brilliant 24-win Cy Young Award-winning campaign in 1996. Name this pair of right-handers.

76. If you're a fan of this team, there are two fairly safe bets you can make each year—they're not going to win the pennant, and they're not going to finish in last place. Since divisional play kicked off in 1969, they've finished in the basement only twice but are still looking for their first pennant. They've made it to the playoffs six times, but have gotten knocked off in the first round every time. Finishing at or near .500 is par for this team's course—from 1969–99, they've finished at 81–81 four times, 83–79 once, 82–80 three times, 80–82 twice, and 79–83 twice. Name this team that's never the best and rarely the worst.

77. Fifty World Series games were played in the 1990s, and only two pitchers threw complete game shutouts. One was a 10-inning gem in the seventh game of a Series; the other was thrown by a pitcher whose team lost the previous game, 15–14. Can you name these hurlers who threw goose eggs in the Fall Classic? And take an extra point if you get this one: There were five other World Series shutouts in the 1990s in which the starting pitcher did not go the distance. Two of the games were started and won by the same man. Who is it?

78. The NFL has seen its share of franchise moves in recent years, with the Rams vacating Los Angeles in favor of St. Louis, the Browns breaking the hearts of the fans in Cleveland by packing up and going to Baltimore, and Al Davis moving his Raiders from Oakland to Los Angeles and then back to Oakland 13 years later. Baseball has been much more stable. Four expansion teams have been added in the 1990s, but a franchise hasn't changed cities in more than 25 years. Franchise moves were more prevalent in the '40s, '50s, and '60s. Here are five true-false questions on this subject.

    A. After the 1941 season, the St. Louis Browns moved to Baltimore and became the Orioles.
    B. The Athletics spent 25 years in Kansas City before they moved to Oakland in 1968.
    C. The Mariners were not the first major league baseball team to play in Seattle.
    D. After the 1971 season, the Senators left the nation's capital and headed to Texas.
    E. Atlanta fans were treated to big league baseball for the first time in 1966 when the club's ownership moved the Braves from Milwaukee.

79. These players share the same first and last names as famous musicians, actors, and football players. Identifying them shouldn't be much of a strain.

    A. The career of this relief pitcher started out slowly, but has picked up steam over the years; he had his best season in 1998 when he saved 40 and posted a 1.55 ERA. Conversely, hits like "Billie Jean" and "Don't Stop 'til You Get Enough" launched this musician into superstardom at a young age, but he's been embroiled in some controversy since.
    B. This outfielder played briefly for the Cardinals in 1995 and 1996. A few years earlier, his namesake picked apart the defenses of the Minnesota Vikings, Dallas Cowboys, and Los Angeles Rams in Super Bowls.
    C. He has won 16 or more games in a season for the Rangers and A's. A musician with the same name has heard mostly cheers from his adoring crowds as he's belted out hit

songs like "Lady" and "She Believes in Me."

D. Two players who had brief careers with the 1980 Braves and 1991 Astros share the same name as an actor who played a great baseball player in a 1942 movie.

80. When Mitch was with the Cubs, he used to get some golfing in with his teammates, especially during spring training in Arizona. One of the Cubs was the best golfer Mitch ever walked the fairway with. Another Cub is the son of an outfielder who was one of two players traded for Hank Aaron. Match these Cub teammates of Mitch's with the brief bits of information we've provided.

Greg Maddux	**A.** Father was traded for Hank Aaron
Derrick May	**B.** Had three stints with the Padres; also played for the White Sox and Tigers before joining the Cubs
Paul Assenmacher	**C.** In top 15 on all-time games pitched list
Luis Salazar	**D.** Best golfer Mitch ever played with
Calvin Schiraldi	**E.** Lost Games 6 and 7 of 1986 World Series

81. If you can answer this one without any hints, you really know your stuff. If you don't get it right off, though, try the hints, one at a time, and eventually you ought to nail it. Who is the only player to collect 500 hits for four different teams? If you can't think of it, these clues should help: 1) He also hit 50 or more home runs for each of the four teams. 2) He played in the majors from 1963 to 1985. 3) The Tigers were the only American League team among the four. 4) For three of the teams, he played in at least one All-Star Game; for the fourth, the Mets, he played in a World Series. 5) He was nicknamed "Le Grand Orange."

82. Hank Aaron never did it. Willie Mays never did it. Neither did Ted Williams nor Reggie Jackson. In fact, in the history of baseball, the feat of banging out 100 extra base hits in a season has been accomplished just eight times. One player, in the 1930s, did it twice with 107 extra base hits in 1930 and 103 in 1932. An active player turned the trick in 1995 when he hammered 52 doubles, one triple, and 50 home runs. He came within a whisker of hitting the century mark again in 1998, as he finished with 99. Can you pick out the old-timer who reached the 100-extra base hit plateau twice, and the active slugger who has almost done it twice?
   A. Al Simmons and Barry Bonds
   B. Chuck Klein and Albert Belle
   C. Hank Greenberg and Greg Vaughn
   D. Lou Gehrig and Ken Griffey Jr.
   E. Hack Wilson and Juan Gonzalez

83. June 23, 1971. Riverfront Stadium in Cincinnati. It was the scene of one of baseball's most impressive one-game performances ever. That night, a right-hander for the Phillies threw a no-hitter against the Reds, allowing just one walk, *and* he hit two home runs. When he came to bat in the ninth inning, Cincinnati fans showed their class by giving him a standing ovation. Two months later, he hit two home runs in a game again, although this time he didn't toss a no-hitter. He won a very respectable 188 games in his career, but he didn't win nearly as many as the pitcher for whom he was traded even-up after the 1971 season. Name this hurler whom the Phillies brought up from the minors in 1964 when he was only 18.

84. Mitch may have walked a few batters in his day, but at least he never led the league in walks allowed. Here are questions about four pitchers who did.
   A. He led his league in walks *eight* times and is the all-time leader in walks allowed, with 962 more than the number-two man.
   B. This fireballer, who was one of the players who roomed with Mitch on the road when he was with the Rangers, was very wild in his early years, and he led the American League in walks in 1986, 1987, and 1989.

C. Winner of 185 games, this right-hander led the league in walks for three different teams, the Orioles (1975), Red Sox (1979), and Mets (1983).

D. He set the single-season record for walks allowed which still stands with 208 for the 1938 Indians. He later threw three no-hitters.

85. The attrition rate always seems high for major league managers, not just Yankees skippers. For example, since 1987, both the Angels and Cubs have changed managers about once every other year. It's so hard to hold on to a managerial job for a long time that, in this century, only four managers have piloted the same team in 20 consecutive seasons. Connie Mack is the hands-down winner—he was at the helm of the Philadelphia A's for 50 straight years (1901–50). Fiery John McGraw managed the New York Giants for 31 years running (1902–32). The other two field bosses managed the same team, one after the other. The first piloted the team for 23 years, retired, and then his successor took over and held the job for 19½ years before health problems forced him to step down. Name these managers who never got the pink slip.

86. In addition to Mitch, the Phillies have had their share of good relievers over the years. Here are questions about four.

A. He became the first reliever to be voted MVP when he won 16 and notched 22 saves to help "The Whiz Kids" edge the Dodgers for the pennant in 1950.

B. This popular lefty pitched out of the Phillies bullpen for 10 years and was the team's leader in saves four times. His high point came in the 1980 World Series when he won one and saved two, including the decisive sixth game against the Royals. Rumor has it that once when he was asked how he spent his money, he responded jokingly, "Ninety percent I spend on wine, women, and song; the other 10 percent I waste."

C. The Phils were back in the World Series in 1983, and this hard-throwing southpaw was one of the reasons. "Mr. T." saved 25 and struck out 100 batters in 93 innings.

D. The 1987 Phillies finished with a losing record, but this bearded flame-thrower piled up 40 saves on his way to the Cy Young Award.

87. It seems like an eternity since Tom Seaver was humming his fastballs by major league hitters, but actually it was recently enough that eight players active in 1999 were teammates of his. Two played with Tom Terrific for the 1983 Mets; four played with him when he was on the White Sox from 1984 through the middle of the 1986 season; and the other two were teammates of his on the Red Sox the second half of the 1986 season, Seaver's last in the majors. Two of these players saw action for the Yankees in 1999, two played for the Orioles (although one was traded to the Indians in August), and the other four played for the Braves, Mets, Devil Rays, and Rockies. You should get five or six with relative ease; seven or eight would be commendable.

88. Except for the 1998 Yankees, the 1995 Indians' winning percentage of .694 (100–44) is the highest for a team since 1954. As a team, the Tribe hit a scorching .291. They scored nearly six runs per game, and seven of their regulars hit at least .300. We'll provide the positions and batting averages of the seven, and you ought to be able to fill out all or most of the Indians' lineup that year.

Position	Batting Average
Catcher	.300 (Injuries limited him to 203 at bats.)
Second base	.314
Third base	.314
Left field	.317
Center field	.310
Right field	.308
Designated hitter	.323

89. Remember the cannon arm of Ellis Valentine? He used to nail runners at the plate with those strikes from right field. But do you remember the team for whom he played most of his career? Mike Boddicker's "foshball" (combination forkball and change-up) helped him win 134 games for four big league teams. Whom did he play for the longest? For Valentine, Boddicker, and three other players, we've listed the four teams they played for in their careers. Pick the one for whom each played the most games.

Player	Teams
Ellis Valentine	Expos, Mets, Angels, Rangers
Andy Van Slyke	Cardinals, Pirates, Orioles, Phillies
Terry Kennedy	Cardinals, Padres, Orioles, Giants
Bruce Hurst	Red Sox, Padres, Rockies, Rangers
Mike Boddicker	Orioles, Red Sox, Royals, Brewers

90. What a shame that Mr. Cub, Ernie Banks, who used to chirp happily on sunny days in Chicago, "It's a good day to play two," never had the good fortune to play in a World Series. He wasn't the only star player who was denied the opportunity to show his stuff in the Fall Classic. Each pair of players below includes a player who played in at least one World Series and one who didn't. Tell us which one played in the Series—and for whom, if you can remember—and which always had to watch the Series on TV.
  A. Juan Marichal, Phil Niekro
  B. Jim Perry, Gaylord Perry
  C. Ferguson Jenkins, Luis Tiant
  D. Rod Carew, Robin Yount
  E. Dave Winfield, Andre Dawson

91. What a boost to the ego it must be when a team trades six players for you. That's what a pitcher felt when the Giants traded Dave Heaverlo, John Johnson, Alan Wirth, Gary Alexander, Gary Thomasson, and Mario Guerrero for him in March 1978. Can you name the pitcher? And while you're at it, see if you can name these men who were each swapped for at least four other players.
  A. The Phillies thought so much of this tall, lean, left-handed hitter's ability that they traded five players, including Manny Trillo and Julio Franco, to acquire him from the Indians after the 1982 season.
  B. The Yankees traded Eric Milton, Danny Mota, Brian Buchanan, and Cristian Guzman—and George Steinbrenner chipped in a reported three million dollars—to pick up this player just before the start of spring training in 1998. He contributed to the Yankees' historic 125-win season.
  C. The Mets received this star following the 1984 season in exchange for Hubie Brooks, Herm Winningham, Mike Fitzgerald, and Floyd Youmans, and he helped them to their World Championship in 1986.

92. Here's one for you fans to debate: Who has been a better pitcher, smoke-throwing Roger "The Rocket" Clemens or Mr. Finesse, Greg Maddux? Through 1999, which pitcher has...
  A. won more Cy Young Awards?
  B. led his league in innings pitched more?
  C. won more post-season games?
  D. walked fewer batters per nine innings in his career?
  E. won more strikeout titles?
  F. a better career winning percentage?
  G. won more Gold Gloves?
  H. had more 20-win seasons?
  I. won an MVP?
  J. a better career ERA?

93. "The Big Train," Walter Johnson, won eight straight strikeout titles, Babe Ruth rattled off seven consecutive slugging crowns, and Rogers Hornsby led the league in hitting six years running, but in the history of baseball, no player has ever won more than three RBI titles in a row. In fact, since the 1930s, only two players have won the RBI crown three straight years, one in each league. The National Leaguer did it in the mid-1970s; one of the years, he hit 52 home runs. The American Leaguer had his run in the early 1990s, and he socked 51 home runs one of those seasons. He was playing in the majors as recently as 1998, while the National Leaguer called it quits in 1986. Name these RBI titlists.

94. See how long it takes you to name this player. He had 40–home run seasons in the 1960s and 1980s, but didn't have one in the 1970s. Trust us, though, he wasn't slacking off in the 1970s—he had some of his finest moments that decade.

95. Not since financial pressures forced Philadelphia A's manager Connie Mack to sell many of his star players after their pennant-winning 1914 season—and then finish 43–109 in 1915—did a team fall as fast as the Florida Marlins. After spending $89 million on free agents, owner Wayne Huizenga watched his Marlins win the 1997 World Series, and then, because the team was losing millions, he traded several of his best players in the off-season and early in the 1998 season. Manager Jim

Leyland looked on helplessly as the Marlins limped home with a 54–108 record. We've given you the basics on some of the key trades: the player's position, team to whom he was traded, and date of the swap. You name the players.

Position	Team	Date
Starting left fielder	Astros	November 11, 1997
Closer	Giants	November 18, 1997
Starting center fielder	Diamondbacks	November 19, 1997
Starting pitcher	Padres	December 15, 1997
Starting pitcher	Mets	February 6, 1998
Starting third baseman	Dodgers	May 15, 1998
Starting right fielder	Dodgers	May 15, 1998
Starting catcher	Dodgers	May 15, 1998
Reserve outfielder	Dodgers	May 15, 1998

96. Next time you peruse a list of major league players and their birthplaces, take note what a large percentage of players hail from California, Puerto Rico, and the Dominican Republic. You'll also see no shortage of players from Florida, Arizona, New York, and Connecticut. What you won't see are many players from Alaska, Hawaii, and Australia—but there are some. Match these players with their unusual birthplaces.

Curt Schilling   **A.** Honolulu, Hawaii
Dave Nilsson   **B.** Brisbane, Queensland, Australia
Chili Davis   **C.** Würzburg, West Germany
Ron Darling   **D.** Anchorage, Alaska
Mike Blowers   **E.** Kingston, Jamaica

97. A few players have racked up 1000 hits for two different teams, but we're only going to concentrate on one here. He got his first 1000 for the Indians in the 1970s, was traded to the Rangers, and he picked up his 1000th hit for them in the 1980s. He retired in 1989 with 201 home runs—five more and he would have caught his father. He managed for the better part of three years in the 1990s. Name this infielder with a career hit total of 2514.

98. When you're sipping your morning coffee and reading the sports section, you'll usually see lists of league leaders in runs scored and runs batted in. But you'll rarely see the leaders in a category that is arguably more important—runs produced, which is calculated by adding a player's runs and RBIs and subtracting his home runs—because if a player hits a home run, he gets credited with a run scored and an RBI for knocking in himself (plus one for each runner on base), but only produces one run (plus a run for each baserunner). Lou Gehrig holds the record for most runs produced in a season with 301, which he set in 1931 when he scored 163 runs, drove in 184, and hit 46 home runs, but he's not the all-time leader in that category. Who do you suppose is?

99. His critics argued that he managed 17 years in the majors and only reached the post-season once, despite having several star-studded teams. His supporters hailed him as "a great motivator" and "the eternal optimist" who guided his team to a World Championship, rebounding from a 3–1 deficit to win the World Series. Two other noteworthy facts about him: He had an excellent rapport with controversial slugger Dick Allen; and while he was managing, he was *traded*—for catcher Manny Sanguillen following the 1976 season. Name this skipper.

100. With the addition of the Tampa Bay Devil Rays and Arizona Diamondbacks in 1998, baseball expanded for the sixth time in 38 years, which has increased the total teams in the majors from 16 to 30. It started in 1961 when the American League added the Los Angeles Angels and Washington Senators. Two more teams were added in 1962, four in 1969, and two more in 1977, 1993, and 1998. Some teams turned into winners almost immediately (in addition to the Diamondbacks, one team had a winning record its second year in existence), while other teams struggled for years before they could shake their losing ways. (It took one expansion team 15 years before it posted a winning record.) Match these expansion teams with the number of seasons it took them to field a winning team.

Seattle Mariners   **A.** 9
Montreal Expos   **B.** 15
Los Angeles Angels   **C.** 11
Washington Senators   **D.** 7
Toronto Blue Jays   **E.** 2

SLIDERS DOWN AND IN

Who Am I?

101. I was about as slow as Mitch was wild. So slow that my Rangers teammates in the mid-1980s nicknamed me "Sluggo." So slow that I stole 18 bases in 16 major league seasons. But I was a tough, hard-nosed catcher who could hit, especially during my six years in Pittsburgh. From 1990 to 1995, I hit .305 as a part-time backstop for the Bucs, including a .345 mark in 1992 in 255 at bats, which was the highest average for a catcher in more than 30 years until Mike Piazza came along. And I was smart, too—I have a degree in economics from UCLA. Who am I?

102. Damon Berryhill and I did most of the catching during Mitch's two seasons in the Windy City, which were my first two years in the majors. Mitch sized up my defense at that time accurately when he said that I had a strong arm, but my ability to call a game and handle pitchers needed improvement. I've worked hard on those aspects of my game over the years, and Mitch has noticed a significant improvement—he thinks I'm one of baseball's best defensive catchers these days. Andy Pettitte, David Cone, Mariano Rivera, and the rest of the Yankees pitchers, whom I've caught in recent years, would undoubtedly agree. While I'm not much of an offensive threat usually, in the 1996 World Series against the Braves, I came through with a key RBI-triple off Greg Maddux in the decisive sixth game, which helped us win, 3–2. Also in 1996, I set the Yankee record for stolen bases in a season by a catcher with 13, breaking the old mark established by the immortal Ed Sweeney in 1910. Who am I?

103. I sat in the Phillies bullpen with Mitch in the 1993 season pondering weighty questions like "What was the best thing *before* sliced bread?" and "Why is it that we drive on the parkway and park on the driveway?" I was used primarily as a set-up man, keeping the other team at bay in the eighth before Mitch came in and closed the door in the ninth. Ten years before pitching in the 1993 World Series against the Blue Jays, I pitched for the Phillies in the World Series against the Orioles. In between my two stints in Philadelphia, I pitched for the Astros, Red Sox, and Padres. Who am I?

104. Mitch sounded like a scout when he said that I had superstar written all over me when I broke into the majors with the 1986 Rangers. Like Mitch, I made it to the Bigs at a young age: 20. My rookie year was a learning experience for me, but by my sophomore year, I was tearing up the league—I hit 30 home runs and drove in 109 runs. And in 1989, I led the American League with 119 RBIs. I could hit for average, too. For the Rangers in 1991, I reached the 200-hit mark, as did Rafael Palmiero and

Julio Franco, and in so doing we became the third trio of teammates in the last half-century to collect 200 hits each. My stock as a slugger remained high into the mid 1990s, as I was on opposite ends of trades for boppers Jose Canseco, Danny Tartabull, and Cecil Fielder. But I slowly began to lose my stroke, and following the 1996 season, I was traded for the considerably less well-known Decomba Conner and Ben Bailey. Who am I?

105. Like Sandy Koufax, I was born in Brooklyn and concentrated more on basketball than baseball when I was growing up. My last two years of high school, I didn't play baseball but was an All-American basketball player, using my six-foot-seven height to pull down a lot of rebounds. Much like how Sandy chose baseball when the Dodgers offered him a contract, I forewent basketball in favor of pitching when the Pirates signed me to a contract in 1973. Although I didn't skip the minors like Sandy, I ascended to the majors rapidly—I was in the Bucs starting rotation in 1975 and remained there for about a decade. I was probably the club's steadiest pitcher during that time, routinely finishing in the top three on the staff in wins and innings pitched. My best year was 1977: I was 20–5 and led the National League with a 2.34 ERA. In the middle of the disastrous 1985 season in which the Pirates would finish 57–104, the team traded me to the Angels. I had to pack my bags often the rest of my career; the best pitching I did after I left Pittsburgh was as a short reliever for the Dodgers for two years in the early 1990s. Who am I?

106. Most guys spend their summer after they turn 16 pumping gas, painting houses, or cutting grass—I spent mine playing minor league baseball. The Yankees drafted me when I was 15, and I was pitching in the minors by the following year. I quickly worked my way up through their system, and by 1984, still a teenager, I was pitching at Yankee Stadium. They traded me to the A's after that season in a mammoth trade involving Rickey Henderson, and in 1986, still not 21, I struck out 16 Mariners in a game. I was inconsistent with the A's, though, and they sent me to the Reds after the 1987 season, and it was in Cincy that I came into my own. My ERA was less than 3.00 six straight years, and I won 13 or more games all but one of those years; I would have won more had I not been hampered by frequent injuries. In 1990, I was named World Series MVP as I won two games against my old team, the A's, allowing one run in 15⅓ innings. In 1993, I led the National League in strikeouts. The nasty slider that I threw took its toll on my elbow, and in 1995 I underwent reconstructive surgery similar to that which Tommy John underwent years earlier. While Tommy was able to bounce back and pitch for several years after the surgery, I was not—1995 was my final year. Still, my career was good, as I won 111 games, and my strikeout per nine inning ratio of 7.84 was better than that of Steve Carlton, Bob Gibson, and my ex-father-in-law, Juan Marichal. Who am I?

107. I've turned into one of baseball's best sluggers, and for that I owe a debt of gratitude to, would you believe, Robert Redford. The legendary actor played Roy Hobbs in the 1984 movie *The Natural*, based on Bernard Malamud's novel. My hitting coach, Charlie Manuel, was watching the movie in the clubhouse, and noticed that Redford, batting left-handed, was using an unorthodox hitting style. While the pitcher was getting the sign from the catcher and starting to go into his windup, he held the bat with his right hand, waving it back and forth, and then just before the pitcher delivered the ball, he would grip the bat with his left hand and get ready to unleash his left-handed swing. Manuel suggested that I try it, and I did—and it has worked wonders for me. I hit 38 home runs in 1996, 40 in 1997 plus two in the post-season, and 30 in 1998, plus six in the post-season, including a grand slam and 33 in 1999 plus four in the post-season, including another slam. Who am I?

108. I went straight from Oklahoma State star to the Rangers starting lineup in 1986. Because I had never played in the minors, I was pretty green when I got to the big leagues, and I fell victim to a lot of pranks by the Rangers players. For example, one of my teammates would be eating an ice cream cone, complain that it didn't smell right, and ask me if I'd take a whiff. Being a nice guy, I would—and I'd end up wearing the ice cream. My way of retaliating was to victimize American League pitchers for home runs, which I did 30 times that season. I spent five years in Texas, and after that was a part-time outfielder/desig-

nated hitter who played all over the map from Houston to Detroit to Chiba Lotte of the Japanese League. My most memorable season was in 1993; platooning in left field for the Phillies, I blasted 24 home runs and drove in 89 runs in 368 at bats to help Mitch, Dutch, The Dude, and company to the National League pennant. Who am I?

109. Lucky for me, I don't mind filling out Change of Address forms at the post office. I've sure had enough practice. Between the minors and the majors, I've pitched on 19 different teams through 1999. Peninsula of the Carolina League (1983), Maine of the International League (1987–88), and Albuquerque of the Pacific Coast League (1990) are some of my minor league stops. My major league resumé includes time with the Mets (1993–94), Red Sox (1995–96), and Expos (1998). While my career has been long, it's hardly been sensational. I've neither won nor saved 10 games in a season. I was primarily a starter earlier in my career, but have been used mostly as a middle reliever in recent years. My best years to date have been with the Padres in 1991 and 1992 when I recorded ERAs of 2.46 and 2.37. My 1999 season was standard fare for me: one win, one loss, no saves, and a 3.77 ERA. All this mediocrity would be easier to take if my little brother wasn't having himself a Hall-of-Fame career. Who am I?

110. Norm Charlton was nicknamed "The Genius" because he graduated from Rice University with a triple major. Randy Myers was nicknamed "Mr. Mellow" because he thought he was mellow compared to Charlton and me. Yeah, right. He used to do stuff like fish a half-dead water moccasin out of a pond and bring it inside, and ride around the clubhouse on a mini-bike. And they called me "The Officer" after a Saturday-morning cartoon character. Together, we were known as "The Nasty Boys" when we pitched out of the bullpen for the Reds in the early 1990s. We may have clowned around off the field, but we were all business on the mound. Everybody took his turn leading the Reds in saves. Myers paced the staff in 1990 with 31 saves, I nailed down the same number in 1991 to lead the club, and Charlton saved 26 to top the Reds staff in 1992. I also ranked high in strikeouts per nine innings and number of times suspended. In my six years in Cincinnati, I struck out more than 12 batters per nine innings, and was suspended several times for minor infractions like throwing at batters and fighting. Who am I?

111. The following is not a typographical error: I put together a 58-game hitting streak. Don't worry, Joe DiMaggio fans, because I compiled my streak in college for Oklahoma State, and while it established an NCAA record, The Yankee Clipper's record 56-game streak remains intact. *The Sporting News* named me College Player of the Year in both 1987 and 1988, and when I left Oklahoma State, I played for the United States Olympic team in Seoul. So by the time I stepped on the major league diamond, I had accomplished a lot. I've been no slacker in the Bigs, either. Through 1999, I've had six 20–home run seasons and seven 90-RBI seasons. I made it into the record books in 1995 when I became the eighth player in history to hit two grand slams in one game. I can throw some leather at you also—I've won a bundle of Gold Gloves for my defense at third base. Who am I?

112. I never won a Gold Glove, but Mitch still thought—mostly because of my great range and strong arm—that I was the best defensive third baseman he played with. He and I were teammates with the Rangers for three years until he was traded to the Cubs; I remained in Texas for almost three years before they dealt me to Pittsburgh late in the 1991 season. The Bucs sent me packing to the Cubs in the middle of the 1992 season, and I had the pleasure of playing in Wrigley for three years. I didn't hit much for average—my .272 mark for the Cubs in 1993 was the highest in my career—but I hit 15 or more home runs five times. I was picked by the White Sox in the first round (ninth player) of the 1979 draft following a banner high school career at Servite High in Anaheim, California, where I played with Mike Witt, who later pitched for the Angels and Yankees. I bypassed the minors and instead attended Stanford University, where I helped the baseball team advance to the College World Series in 1982. Because of my success on the baseball diamond, I was kind of a "big man on campus" at Stanford, but not as much as my roommate John Elway. Who am I?

113. In 1989, I led the majors in two important categories: home runs by a catcher and bowls of Froot Loops eaten. Early in the season, I had a bowl of Loops for breakfast and hit a home run that night, so I kept eating them throughout the season and finished with 26 homers. I cut back on my Froot Loops consumption after that season, but the home runs kept coming. I banged out 30 three times for the Tigers in the early 1990s and the Rangers in 1995. Other categories in which I consistently ranked high: walks and strikeouts—I had five 100-walk seasons and seven 100-K years. Categories in which I regularly ranked low: stolen bases and batting average—I never stole more than three bases in a season, nor hit higher than .263. Who am I?

114. Mitch and the gang on the Phillies used to call me kiddingly "Mikey" because they thought I had two different personalities. I was easygoing hours before a game, but as game time approached, look out—I became very serious and intense.

It was the best of times for me in Philly as I drove in 93 runs in both 1992 and 1993, although I was criticized somewhat for my erratic defense at third base. I have this rifle arm, but once in a while I would sail one over the first baseman's head. The Phillies swapped me to the American League in 1995, and I've played for a few teams since, including the Twins, Angels, and Blue Jays. Who am I?

115. I struck out frequently, was injury prone, and had the reputation of being moody, but when my name was in the lineup, I rang up the scoreboard with a lot of home runs and RBIs. I had five 100-RBI seasons—three with the Royals, one with the Yankees, and one with the White Sox. Among my 262 homers were 11 grand slams, which places me ahead of Willie Mays, Mickey Mantle, and Mike Schmidt on the career slam list. I was an infielder throughout my minor league career, but in the majors I played mostly outfield, the same position that my father played for three American League teams in the 1960s. Speaking of fathers, Mitch's dad cracked a funny line after a home run I hit in 1986. The first time that Mitch's parents saw him pitch in the majors was a game against the Mariners in Seattle that year. Mitch was hoping to pitch well that night in front of the folks, maybe set down the side in the ninth for a save. Giving up back-to-back home runs that traveled a combined 916 feet was not exactly what he had in mind. Jim Presley, our third baseman, started the fireworks off Mitch by hitting one 452 feet into the left field bleachers. I didn't want Jim to outdo me, so I hit the next pitch 464 feet. After the game, Mitch's father kidded Mitch, "God, can you throw the ball a long way!" Who am I?

116. When you look at my season-by-season home run totals, you'll swear there must be a mistake. In my first 1081 big league at bats spread over four years, I hit 10 home runs—not Ruthian numbers by a long shot. I picked up the pace the next four years by hitting 21, 13, 12, and 16 dingers, clearly establishing myself as a hitter with moderate but not great power. But wait. In 1996, out of nowhere, I jacked out 30 homers—*by the All-Star break*—and added 20 more the second half of the season to put me in the 50–home run club with bashers like Hack Wilson, Johnny Mize, and Hank Greenberg. I added three more in the post-season, although we went down in the League Championship

Series. I was back to earth in 1997 when I hit 18 home runs, and matched that figure in 1998, and hit 24 in 1999. My speed also bears mentioning: I stole 53 bases in 1992, which makes me the only player with a 50-home run season and 50-stolen base season. Red Sox fans may recall that I broke in with them in 1988, but mid-season, Curt Schilling and I were traded to another team, for which I had my big home run season. Who am I?

117. Mitch put it best: I didn't look like a ballplayer, I didn't act like a ballplayer, but I could fall out of bed on Christmas Day and get four hits. Starting in 1982, when I finished second in the American League Rookie of the Year vote, year in and year out over the next several seasons I could be counted on to hit between .275 and .315 and bang out 20 or more homers. I finished with 293 round-trippers to rank second on the Twins' all-time list behind Harmon Killebrew. It was fitting that I played my entire career in Minnesota because I grew up down the street from Metropolitan Stadium, where the Twins used to play before moving to the Metrodome. Who am I?

118. Since 1950, six pitchers, including Sandy Koufax, Bob Gibson, and Jim Palmer, have thrown 10 shutouts in a season, and I'm one of them. The way my year began with the Cardinals in 1985, I was having trouble winning any games, let alone throwing shutouts. I opened up 1–7, and then in a dramatic turnaround, won 20 of my last 21 decisions; half of those were by shutout. I added a whitewash in Game 4 of the World Series against the Royals. But 1985 was an aberration for me, especially in the shutouts department. I only blanked the other team six times besides 1985, but I won 13 games two seasons for the Red Sox before I came to St. Louis, and 13 in 1986 for the Cardinals. Arm woes relegated me to the disabled list much of my final five years, but I still finished with impressive career stats: a .619 winning percentage (117–72) and a 3.12 ERA. If sportswriters put together a team of players that they most disliked, I'd be disappointed if I weren't one of the starting pitchers. One of the outfielders, undoubtedly, would be a guy that I was involved in a trade with in 1984: George Hendrick. I was different from him, though. I argued with and insulted writers; old George just didn't talk to them. Who am I?

119. You never know, I might have had a shot at a football career if I had pursued it. After all, I was an All-American quarterback in high school in Oklahoma City, but when the Brewers offered me a fat bonus to sign with them in 1970, I kissed football goodbye. I held down the Brewers starting catching job for four years in the mid-1970s, not hitting much for average, but showing some occasional power. The Brewers sent me to Kansas City following the 1976 season, and for Whitey Herzog's Royals in 1979 I had myself what sportswriters like to call a "career year." I hit .291 with 20 home runs, scored 101 runs, drove in 112, drew a league-leading 121 walks, and even hit 10 triples. I wish I could say that was the first of many 100-RBI seasons, but actually I never drove in even 70 runs again, but at least I got a World Series ring playing for Whitey's 1982 Cardinals. I closed things out with the Rangers in 1986 and 1987 where I caught some of Mitch's smoke his first two years. Who am I?

120. At six-foot-seven and roughly 230 pounds, my legs were big, my shoulders were big, and as Mitch liked to kid me, my head was big. He used to tell me that somewhere there must be

a buffalo with a human head. Mitch got those digs in when we were pitching together for the Cubs in 1989 and 1990. I was 16–11 for the 1989 team, which beat out the Mets by six games for the National League Eastern Division title. Five years earlier, I came to the Cubbies from the Indians in a mid-season trade; in the final three and a half months of the year I went on a rampage, rattling off 14 straight wins en route to a Cy Young Award-winning 16–1 season, and in the process led the Cubs to their first post-season appearance in 39 years. Both years, unfortunately, we lost in the playoffs. One of my prouder achievements came in a 1988 game with the Cubs. No, I didn't throw a no-hitter, nor did I strike out 17 batters. I stole home, which if you haven't noticed, is sort of rare for a pitcher. Who am I?

Mixed Bag

121. After winning 10 pennants and seven World Series for the star-studded Yankees from 1949 to 1960, Casey Stengel boldly accepted the job to manage the Mets their maiden season in 1962. The Mets finished the year 40–120, *60½* games behind the pennant-winning Giants. About the futility of his team, Stengel quipped after the season, "No one man could have done all this." We thought it might be kind of harsh if we asked you questions about Hot Rod Kanehl, Choo Choo Coleman, and Vinegar Bend Mizell, so how about a few on some of the '62 Mets' better-known players?

    A. This future Hall-of-Famer, who won two batting titles for the Phillies in the 1950s, led the Mets with a .306 average and 12 steals. He had the knack of fouling off pitches at will, and prior to a Phillies–Cubs game, one of the Cubs players asked him if he would be kind enough to drill the Cub's ex-wife who was going to be sitting in the stands. In one of his at bats, the Phillie fouled one in the vicinity of the ex-wife, and the Cubs player yelled from third base, "Three rows down!"

    B. What a trouper this pitcher was—he endured 24 losses for Casey's boys, the most in a season by a pitcher since 1935. The next season he showed improvement by only losing 22. He later managed the Giants for seven years from the mid-1980s to the early 1990s.

    C. He was the star of this woeful team with 34 home runs and 94 RBIs. All told, he banged out 286 home runs in his 16-year career.

    D. He provided some comic relief for his teammates—both on and off the field. In a game against the Cubs in June, he hit an apparent two-run triple. The Cubs appealed on the ground that he missed first base, and the umpire agreed and called him out. When Stengel stormed out of the dugout to argue the call, he was informed that his man also missed *second* base. "Well, I know he didn't miss third," barked an exasperated Casey, "because he's standing on it!"

122. See if you can match these Rangers teammates of Mitch's with the various facts listed:

Scott Fletcher	**A.** Ranks first on the Rangers' all-time games played list
Gary Ward	**B.** Nicknamed "Scooter" because he was so small
Jim Sundberg	**C.** Managed the Rangers the second half of the 1992 season
Toby Harrah	**D.** Also played for the Dodgers, Braves, Mariners, White Sox, and Mets
Tom Paciorek	**E.** Hit 28 home runs for the Twins in 1982

123. Name the year: While Mitch was hurling his heat by Little League batters in Oregon, Mike Hargrove won the American League Rookie of the Year Award for the Rangers; fleet-footed Braves outfielder Ralph Garr won the batting title with a .353 average and also topped the league with 17 triples; and the A's, led by Reggie and Catfish, won their third straight World Series—no team has been champion three years in a row since. An added hint for movie buffs: *The Godfather, Part II* was released.

124. No doubt you know that Nolan Ryan threw seven no-hitters, Steve Carlton won four Cy Young Awards, and Bob Gibson struck out a record 17 batters in Game 1 of the 1968 World Series. But do you know what these great pitchers—and two others from the same era—did not do in their careers?

Nolan Ryan	**A.** Did not win 300 games or strike out 15 batters in a game
Steve Carlton	**B.** Did not win a Cy Young Award or a World Series game
Bob Gibson	**C.** Did not win 300 games
Jim Palmer	**D.** Did not win a Cy Young Award or strike out 15 batters in a game or throw a no-hitter
Don Sutton	**E.** Did not throw a no-hitter

125. Not only did Mark McGwire break the single-season home run record in 1998, he also passed Babe Ruth in career at bats per home run ratio. Babe hit one out of the yard every 11.76 at bats, which looked secure until recent years when Big Mark turned on the steam, averaging a home run every *8.13* at bats

from 1995–99 to reduce his career ratio to 10.83. Nobody else has rivaled these guys, but other players have had excellent ratios. Which of these sluggers had the best career at bats per home run ratio?
   A. Ernie Banks
   B. Willie Stargell
   C. Jim Rice
   D. Johnny Bench
   E. Mitch Williams

126. You heard about a thousand times during the home run chase in 1998 that Roger Maris hit 61 homers in 1961. But how did he fare in his career other than that season? Did he hit 50 homers in a season before or after his record-breaking year? How about 40? Did he hit 400 home runs in his career? 300? What was Roger's second-highest season home run output and lifetime home run total?
   A. 39 and 275
   B. 41 and 341
   C. 43 and 310
   D. 48 and 402
   E. 53 and 368

127. According to the old saying, two is company, but three's a crowd. With regard to brothers playing in the majors, two is common, but three is a rarity. Fewer than two dozen sets of parents have seen three or more of their sons make it to the big leagues. Leading the way with five (Ed, Tom, Jim, Frank, and Joe) were the Delahantys, who played in the late 1800s and early 1900s. We've picked out five three-brother acts and given you the first names of two of the brothers. Your job is to come up with the first name of the third brother and the family's last name.
   A. Vince and Dom
   B. Hank and Ron
   C. Hector and Tommy
   D. Cloyd and Clete
   E. Jesus and Matty

128. There have also been a multitude of father-son combinations who have donned major league uniforms. Only a handful of players, however, sent *two* sons to the majors. Again we've picked out five such families and given you the first names of the two sons. See if you can come up with the father's first name and the family's last name.

- **A.** Aaron and Bret
- **B.** Roberto and Sandy
- **C.** Todd and Mel
- **D.** Andy and Jose
- **E.** John and Jerry

129. How hard is it for a pitcher to win 25 games in a season? Consider this: No active pitcher—not Greg Maddux, nor Randy Johnson, nor Pedro Martinez, nor Roger Clemens—has accomplished the feat. In fact, over the last 20 years of the 20th century, only two pitchers reached the quarter-century mark in victories in a season. The first won 25 in 1980; the second won 27 in 1990. Each was a right-hander who turned the trick in the American League at the age of 33. Each pitched in the National League during his career. Each won 10 more games in his big year than in his next winningest season. Name this pair.

130. Every dog has his day, and every star doesn't always shine. Hank Aaron is the all-time home run leader, Cal Ripken Jr. holds the iron-man streak, and Brooks Robinson set some records with his amazing defense at third base. But Aaron, Ripken, and Robinson, along with Mickey Mantle and Reggie Jackson, each hold at least one record that they would just as soon not. Match the player with the record.

Hank Aaron	**A.** Holds record for most strikeouts in World Series play
Cal Ripken Jr.	**B.** The mark for most double plays grounded into in a career belongs to him
Brooks Robinson	**C.** Set record for most at bats in a season without a triple
Reggie Jackson	**D.** Hit into a record four triple plays
Mickey Mantle	**E.** All-time leader in lifetime K's

131. Unless you've spent the last couple years in Siberia, you know that in 1998 Mark McGwire and Sammy Sosa broke Roger Maris's esteemed record of 61 home runs in a season, which he set in 1961. Even before 1998, we assume that you knew Maris held the record. But we'd be surprised if the names Earl Webb and Owen "Chief" Wilson mean anything to you. They hold the single-season records for doubles and triples in a season. Wilson set the triples record for the Pirates in 1912; Webb established the doubles mark for the Red Sox in 1931. Other than setting those records, neither did much to speak of. Webb played seven years in the majors; Wilson played nine. Aside from his one big season, Webb never led the league in doubles; in fact, his second-highest doubles total was 30. Likewise, the Chief only led the league in triples the year he set the record; his next-highest total in a season was 14. Can you guess how many doubles and triples Webb and Wilson hit in their record-setting seasons?

A. 55 and 31
B. 59 and 38
C. 67 and 36
D. 63 and 26
E. 70 and 29

132. Here are five players who each finished with at least 2100 hits. You'll know the teams they played for/have played for and their positions, but can you tell us from which side of the plate they hit, and whether they throw/threw right- or left-handed. Then try ranking them in career hits.

Rickey Henderson   **A.** Switch-hitter, right-handed thrower
Willie Wilson   **B.** Right-handed hitter, left-handed thrower
Keith Hernandez   **C.** Right-handed hitter, right-handed thrower
Joe Morgan   **D.** Left-handed hitter, left-handed thrower
Ryne Sandberg   **E.** Left-handed hitter, right-handed thrower

133. Talk about pressure: A star player and big fan favorite dies, retires, or falls ill, and a young player has the job of replacing him. Here are descriptions of four players who were asked to fill the shoes of legends.

A. When Lou Gehrig was forced to sit down in 1939 after 2130 straight games because of a disease which would take his life two years later, what player replaced "The Iron Horse," hitting .235 and .264 in his two seasons as the Yanks' first baseman?

B. Red Sox icon Ted Williams bade farewell to Boston in 1960 after a long and illustrious career that began in 1939. Taking over in left field for the Sox was a young left-handed hitter with tremendous potential and an unusual batting stance. How did he do? We'll give you a clue—he got more hits in his career than Ted did.

C. "The Human Vacuum Cleaner" Brooks Robinson won the hearts of Orioles fans for more than 20 years with clutch hitting and remarkable defense at third base. He slowed down late in his career, and his last two seasons, 1976 and 1977, he played part-time, giving way to a young player who had worked his way up through the Orioles minor league organization. Brooks's replacement handled the job commendably, averaging 17 homers and playing good, albeit not Brooks-like, defense, in his six years as the O's starting third baseman. He had a few more good years with the Angels.

D. August 2, 1979, was a sad day for Yankees fans: The team's catcher and captain, Thurman Munson, died while flying his private plane. The following year, the difficult task of taking over the catching job fell to this man, and he handled the pressure admirably. He contributed to the Yankees' division-winning season in 1980 by hitting .277 with 85 RBIs. He remained in pinstripes until 1984, although Butch Wynegar spelled him as number-one catcher in 1983.

134. A handful of players have hit two grand slams in one game, and about two dozen players have hit two home runs in one inning, but it wasn't until April 23, 1999, when a player—Cardinals' third baseman Fernando Tatis—hit two grand slams in

one inning. The only National Leaguer to slug two grand slams in a game before Tatis was a *pitcher*, who accomplished the feat in 1966. He wasn't a bad pitcher, either—he won 113 games with a high of 24 in 1965. Who is he?
- **A.** Chris Short
- **B.** Nelson Briles
- **C.** Larry Jackson
- **D.** Jim Maloney
- **E.** Tony Cloninger

135. What's more exciting, watching Juan Gonzalez or Manny Ramirez go deep, or seeing Kenny Lofton or Tony Womack steal second on a bang-bang play? Because we already have a lot of questions on home run hitters, we're going to ask you about some great base stealers. These would be hanging curveballs if we asked you who the top three all-time base thieves are (Rickey Henderson, Lou Brock, and Ty Cobb; you knew that, right?), so try to answer these questions about four other players in the top 15.
- **A.** This shortstop stole 104 bases for the Dodgers in 1962 to set the single-season record, which Brock broke in 1974.
- **B.** Starting in 1985, he won six straight stolen base titles for the Cardinals, averaging 92 per year with three 100-steal seasons. He's fifth on the career list with 762.
- **C.** He's first among players who never won a stolen base title, with 689 steals.
- **D.** This outfielder pilfered 668 bases, most of them for the Royals in the late 1970s and 1980s.

136. Here's another one about stolen bases. Did you know that there was a player who won the league stolen base title his first *nine* years out of the chute? Yet his lifetime stolen base title of 506 puts him 18th on the list, more than 800 behind leader Rickey Henderson. He didn't walk or strike out much. Is it...
- **A.** Bert Campaneris
- **B.** Luis Aparicio
- **C.** Tommy Harper
- **D.** Cesar Cedeno
- **E.** Omar Moreno

137. Mitch's 85 games pitched for the Rangers in 1987 marked his season high and put him in the top 20 on the all-time list for games by a pitcher in one year. The record is a remarkable 106, which was set by a pitcher in the 1970s; he appeared in 90 or more games two other seasons. There has been one other pitcher who has relieved in 90 plus games three times; one of those years was as a Phillie in the 1980s. Name these two workhorses.
   A. Hoyt Wilhelm and Don Carman
   B. Goose Gossage and Gene Garber
   C. Mike Marshall and Kent Tekulve
   D. Pedro Borbon and Jeff Parrett
   E. Dan Quisenberry and Bill Campbell

138. Hank Aaron, Willie Mays, Frank Robinson, Reggie Jackson, and Willie McCovey. Not a bad collection of sluggers. They rank first, third, fourth, sixth, and tied for tenth on the all-time home run list, and averaged 617 long balls. But none won a home run title until at least his fourth season, none won more than one his first seven years, and none won more than four titles in his career. Yet there is a player, who through the 1999 season ranks a distant 47th on the lifetime home run list with 369, who led or shared the league lead in home runs his first *seven* years in the majors. Two of those seasons, he hit the 50 mark. A back ailment ended his career when he was 32. Who is this slugger?
   A. Duke Snider
   B. Willie Stargell
   C. Joe Adcock
   D. Ralph Kiner
   E. Gil Hodges

139. How times have changed! In recent years, the game has abounded with home run–hitting shortstops like Robin Yount, Cal Ripken Jr., and Alex Rodriguez. But back in the 1960s, as a rule, shortstops were counted on to play good defense, but weren't expected to hit much. For five shortstops of that era (all started their careers in the 1960s and retired between 1972 and 1981), we've given you the teams for whom they played the most games, along with their career batting averages, slugging averages, and home run totals. It's up to you to recall their names.

Team	Batting Average	Slugging Average	Home Runs
A. Orioles	.227	.280	20
B. Senators	.224	.300	60
C. Mets	.236	.288	7
D. Phillies	.215	.286	30
E. Giants	.228	.275	8

140. The first 80 years of the 20th century, perfect games were a rare commodity—only eight pitchers twirled perfectos. But the hurlers picked up the pace over the last two decades by throwing seven—or one approximately every three years. All good pitchers in the group, but it's unlikely that any will go to the Hall. We've given you the year and the team for whom each of the seven pitched the gem.

Year	Team
1981	Cleveland Indians
1984	California Angels
1988	Cincinnati Reds
1991	Montreal Expos
1994	Texas Rangers
1998	New York Yankees
1999	New York Yankees

141. Over the years, a few players have been related by marriage or blood to noteworthy people in other walks of life, athletes and actresses among them. One player's father hosted the long-running TV game show "Hollywood Squares." Another's sister was one of the world's best tennis players. Another was married to an actress whose movie credits include *Executive Decision* and *Father Hood*. Match these ballplayers with their well-known relatives.

Randy Moffitt   **A.** husband of golfer Nancy Lopez
Ray Knight   **B.** son of "Hollywood Squares" host Peter Marshall
Pete LaCock   **C.** brother of actress Christine (if we told you her last name, we'd give it away), she's had roles in more than 20 movies
David Justice   **D.** brother of tennis legend Billie Jean King
Jeff Lahti   **E.** ex-husband of actress Halle Berry

142. Ever since the Mets entered the National League in 1962, they have constantly battled their crosstown rivals, the Yankees, for headlines in the New York papers. Curiously, the teams have made few trades over the years, each perhaps reluctant to make a bad deal and get trashed in the press. Here are questions about four players, who weren't involved in trades between the Yankees and Mets, but played for both teams in their careers.

    A. Still active, he's the only pitcher to date who has been a 20-game winner for both the Mets and Yankees. He also won a Cy Young Award—for the Royals in 1994.

    B. This outfielder played in the World Series for the 1986 Mets as well as the 1996 and 1999 Yankees.

    C. He only played eight games for the Yankees—at the end of the 1977 season (that was his fourth team that year)—but he played five and a half seasons for the Mets and hit 154 home runs. He hit 442 career four-baggers.

D. He was mostly a reserve in his seven-year career, which earned him the nickname of "Supersub." He caused a stir in August 1964 when Yankees manager Yogi Berra chewed him out on the team bus for playing his harmonica. The run-in seemed to incite the apathetic Yankees, in third place at the time, and they rallied to win the pennant. In the World Series against the Cardinals, he filled in for injured shortstop Tony Kubek, starting and leading off all seven games. He played on the other side of the East River in part of 1967 and 1968.

143. Over the years, some of the game's best-known and most colorful managers like Sparky Anderson, Billy Martin, and Tommy Lasorda have guided their teams to World Championships. Sometimes, though, the World Series is won by a team whose skipper, while good, isn't as popular as Sparky, Billy, or Tommy. Here are four such managers who won the Series in the 1980s or 1990s.

A. He led the Phillies to a World Series triumph in 1980 and later managed the Yankees and Mets.

B. He succeeded Earl Weaver as Orioles manager in 1983 and led the Birds to the World Championship his first year.

C. The Royals have only won one World Series to date, in 1985. Their manager, who piloted the Yankees to the division title in 1980 before losing to the Royals in the playoffs, died of a brain tumor in 1987.

D. Some criticized him because he was too soft-spoken and unemotional, but he led the Blue Jays to consecutive World Series victories in 1992 and 1993.

144. Back in the early days of baseball, players used to hit .370 in a season routinely—Ty Cobb did it 12 times, and Rogers Hornsby had eight .370-plus seasons. Similarly, it wasn't uncommon for a player to drive in 150 runs—Lou Gehrig had seven 150-RBI seasons, while Babe Ruth had five. But since 1960, only one player has had a .370 season *and* a 150-RBI season (not in the same year). Name him.

A. Andres Galarraga
B. George Brett
C. Tommy Davis
D. Frank Thomas
E. Roberto Clemente

145. At six-four, Mitch is taller than most major-leaguers, but there have been players he would have to look up to. We've picked out four for your consideration, and because height is the theme of this question, we've added a couple about short players.

    A. Writer George Vecsey said about this six-foot-seven giant, "He hit a baseball farther than a baseball ought to go." He slugged most of his 382 home runs for the Dodgers and Senators in the 1960s and early 1970s.

    B. He was six-eight and threw about as hard as Randy Johnson. He fanned more than 300 for the Astros in 1978 and 1979, but a stroke ended his career in 1980.

    C. At five-foot-four, he was one of the shortest players to grace the baseball diamond. He was a starting shortstop for more than 10 years, mostly for the Royals in the 1970s. He responded to jokes about his height by retorting, "I'd rather be the shortest player in the majors than the tallest in the minors."

    D. If this six-foot, seven-inch right-hander could figure out a way to control his temper, he might be more successful. The last time we checked, he had been tossed out of a game by an umpire for *four* different teams.

    E. He was small (five-six, 160 pounds) and didn't hit much (.221 lifetime with two home runs), but he was a good-fielding reserve shortstop for the Pirates and Braves for 17 years.

    F. How about a medal for this six-foot-eight pitcher's perseverance? He stuck it out in the minors for 14 years before the A's finally gave him the call to the big show in 1994. He assumed the closer role in 1996 and led the team in saves that year as well as the next three seasons. His staff lead in 1999 was especially impressive because the A's traded him with two months left in the season.

146. These two guys must have the same biorhythmns or something. Listen to these similarities. They both bat and throw left-handed. One is six-foot-four, and the other is six-five. They both weigh in the neighborhood of 215 pounds. One played his first eight years in the majors for an American League team and then was traded to a National League team for a guy named Robert. The other played his first eight years in the majors for a National League team and then was traded to an American League team (which plays in the same city as the National League team to whom player number one was traded) for a guy named Roberto. One captured the 1993 American League batting title by hitting .363; the other won the 1994 American League batting title by hitting .359. The single-season home run and RBI highs are 24 and 107 for one and 28 and 117 for the other. One has played for two World Championship teams; the other has played for four. Do the last names of the two players you thought of start with the same letter? If not, you missed at least one.

147. Try to think of a few active players whose last names have 10 or more letters. It's not easy. Nomar Garciaparra, Mark Grudzielanek, and Jeff Montgomery are a few who come to mind. Now try to think of guys with 10-letter last names—or longer—who hit 40 home runs in a season. We counted four, two in the National League, two in the American League. Two did it three times; two did it once. Two had the big home run seasons in the 1950s; two in the 1960s or 1970. Two are in the Hall of Fame; two are not. Can you name them?

148. If you're a diehard baseball fan, undoubtedly you've been poring over players' batting averages in the Sunday paper for years. You always saw Tony Gwynn and Bill Madlock at the top, but where was Enos Cabell? In the .300s, the .230s, or somewhere in between? What about Garry Maddox? "The Secretary of Defense" could chase down a long fly ball to the warning track with the best of them, but could he hit? Here are 10 players who retired in the 1980s or 1990s. Rank them from one to 10 in career batting average.

_____	Steve Braun	_____	Enos Cabell
_____	Garry Maddox	_____	Pedro Guerrero
_____	Cory Snyder	_____	Mario Mendoza
_____	Carney Lansford	_____	Mike Scioscia
_____	Mookie Wilson	_____	Joe Rudi

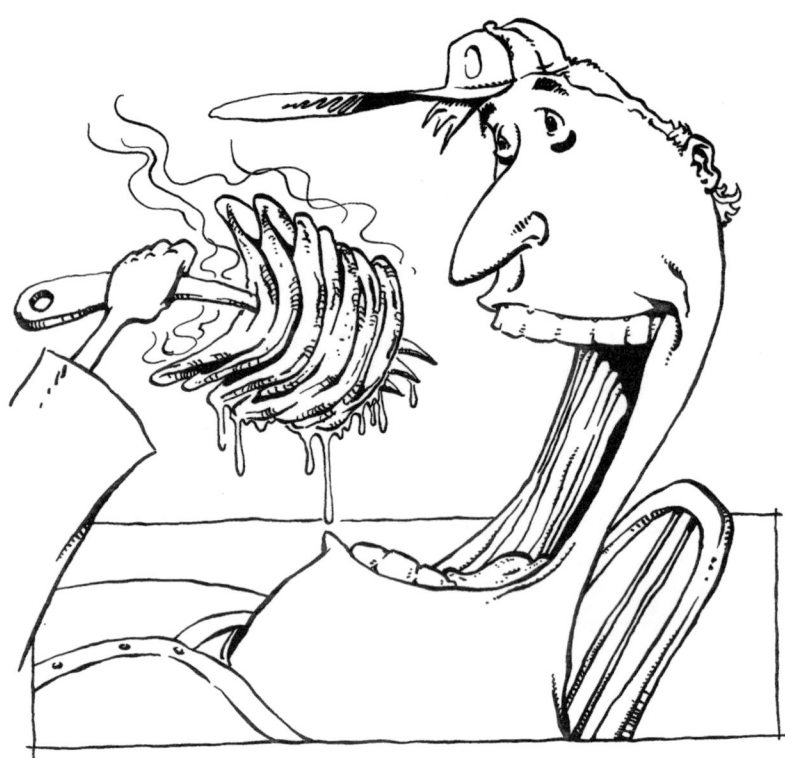

149. In this era of five-man starting rotations, 20-game winners are not that common—usually there are only three or four in the majors each season. But a few years back, they were a dime a dozen. In 1971, for example, 14 hurlers posted 20 or more wins. Here are questions about four of those pitchers who won 20 the year that the Bucs, led by Steve Blass and Roberto Clemente, beat the Orioles in the World Series.

  A. He won 20 for the Dodgers that season, which people tend to forget. After all, this is the unlucky guy who allowed Aaron's 715th home run in April 1974.
  B. This Tigers left-hander won Games 2, 5, and 7 of the 1968 World Series.
  C. In 1971, he recorded the second of his eight 20-win seasons. He liked to eat pancakes on mornings that he pitched.

D. This White Sox knuckleballer pitched a whopping 334 innings in 1971 and came back with 376⅔ more in 1972.

150. In 1999, Sammy Sosa led his Cubs team in home runs for the seventh consecutive season. Impressive stretch by Slammin' Sammy, but a long way from the record. In the first half of the century, a player led his team—the same team—in home runs *18* consecutive seasons. Seven of those seasons, he had at least twice as many homers as the number-two man on the team. He averaged about 28 per year over the 18-year period. He managed the team the last four years. Any idea who it is?

BLAZING FASTBALLS

Who Am I?

151. Mitch has a much higher regard for my brawn than my brain. He described me as "strong as an ox—and damn near as smart as one, too." If you were going to build a rock wall, Mitch says, you'd call me. But if you were going to build a rocket, you'd call somebody else. Like he should talk. Mitch saved some of my 12 wins for the Phillies in 1993 as well as the fourth game of the League Championship Series against the Braves, which we won 2–1. I was no stranger to the post-season—I also hurled for the 1985 Royals and 1990 Reds, who both won the World Series, and the 1992 Pirates, who were the National League Eastern Division Champions. Who am I?

152. Time does fly. It's been more than 30 years since Detroit hosted a ticker-tape parade attended by throngs of rabid Tigers fans after we beat the Cardinals in seven games in the 1968 World Series. Our manager, Mayo Smith, deserves a lot of the credit as he made a risky strategical decision. Although I had less than 70 innings of experience playing shortstop under my belt, he shifted me there for the Series to get Al Kaline's bat in the lineup. He had been a part-time first baseman/outfielder that year, while Willie Horton normally played left field, I played center, and Jim Northrup played right. Mayo's gamble paid off as I got the job done at shortstop, and Kaline was one of the stars of the Series—he hit .379 with two homers and eight RBIs. I played 59 games at short the following season, but for most of my 15-year career, all of which was spent in Detroit, I played the outfield—and quite well, I might add. Who am I?

153. I was a fundamentally sound player, and the person who taught me the basics was not my father, not my older brother, not my Little League coach, it was—please don't laugh—my mother. Back home in the Dominican Republic, my mother, who was an outstanding softball player, taught me the proper batting stance and how to dig low pitches out of the dirt. Mom's advice worked well for me—I played almost two decades in the majors and was regarded as a top defensive catcher. My stick was inconsistent, though; my average ranged from a high of .301 in 1983 to a low of .181 in 1993. My brother Ramon, who was a pitcher, also made it to the majors, but because Mom didn't know much about pitching, he only lasted a year—for the Tigers in 1989. Who am I?

154. I fit in the category of journeyman pitcher. I pitched for six teams in my career, three in each league, including the Cubs in the 1980s before Mitch arrived and for the Rangers in the 1990s after he left. My control was slightly better than Mitch's;

I walked less than 1.5 batters per nine innings in my career, and over a five-year stretch for the Cardinals in the early 1990s, when I was having my winningest seasons, I averaged 1.1 walks per nine innings. In 1992, my control was nearly perfect as I allowed 20 walks in 233 innings. In 1993, it was almost as good: I walked 20 batters in 213⅔ innings and in one stretch, I threw 55 consecutive innings without issuing a walk. Despite my impeccable control, my stats will reflect that I was a mediocre pitcher. I finished my career with a 110–102 record and a 3.92 ERA. Who am I?

155. I was a big fan favorite in Seattle in the Mariners' early years when I smacked 24 home runs in 1977 and 21 in 1979. Some people were predicting greatness for me, but it didn't come to pass, although I had a respectable career, which lasted 12 years and featured time with six teams. Highlights of my career included delivering a pinch-hit triple in the 1982 All-Star Game when I was a Padre and playing for the 1984 World Champion Tigers. Notable lowlights were striking out in eight straight at bats in 1982, which is close to a record for a non-pitcher, and suffering a gut-wrenching League Championship Series loss to the Red Sox in 1986 when I was with the Angels; we led three games to one only to let the Series slip away. It was during that 1986 season when I let Mitch have a piece of my mind. We were playing the Rangers, and Mitch came in to face Reggie Jackson, who was 40 years old at the time. The first pitch Mitch threw was between Reggie's head and helmet, and he hit the deck in a hurry. He dusted himself off, got back in the box, and finished his at bat. The next day, before the game, I saw Mitch in the outfield, ran over to him and demanded, "How can you throw a 95-mile-an-hour fastball at a 40-year-old man's head?!" Mitch told me it wasn't on purpose, but I let him know that if he threw at me, I wasn't going down. I was kidding with Mitch, really; I just had to protect my man Reggie. Who am I?

156. In 1996, my club set the new home run record for a team when we slugged 257 out of the park. (The record lasted all of one year; the Mariners turned around and broke our record in 1997 by hitting 264.) I hit 21 that year to rank *seventh* on my team. At that time, it was a career-high for me, but then I hit 22 in 1998 and 28 in 1999. I played a lot of catcher earlier in my career, then moved to third base, and have been stationed in the outfield in recent years. Before I made it to the majors, I had the honor of playing on the 1984 U.S. Olympic team in Los Angeles. My brother Rich had cups of coffee as a pitcher with the Phillies and Rangers in 1985 and our father, Dick, also had cups of coffee—although longer sips than Rich's—with the NBA's New York Knicks and Milwaukee Hawks for two years in the early 1950s. Who am I?

157. When I was growing up in Kapuskasing, Ontario, I split my time between ripping my slap shot past goalies on the hockey rink and striking out batters on the Little League baseball field. My father, Ted, sparked my interest in hockey—he was a center for the NHL's Minnesota North Stars and WHA's Los Angeles Sharks for three seasons in the late 1960s and early 1970s. I was selected as an All-American hockey player out of the University of Vermont in the 1981 NHL draft by the Winnipeg Jets, and then a year later, the Angels grabbed me in the baseball draft. I

couldn't make up my mind which sport to pursue, so for a while I played minor league baseball and minor league hockey. I finally settled on baseball, and I pitched a dozen years for the Angels and White Sox. My most lasting memories—both good and bad—are from the 1986 season, when I won a career-high 17 for the division-winning Angels, but then got rocked twice in my starts in the playoffs against the Red Sox. After I lost 19 for the Angels in 1991, the White Sox took a chance and signed me as a free agent, hoping I could regain my 1986 regular-season form. I looked like I may be headed in that direction, since I pitched respectably in 1992, finishing second on the team to Jack McDowell with 12 wins. Things then took a turn for the worse. I struggled in 1993 and became a part-time starter, and when my troubles continued in 1994, I was demoted to middle reliever, a role which I performed not particularly well my last three years. Who am I?

158. You want to hear some minor league credentials? In 1985, I was named Appalachian League Player of the Year; in 1986, I won Carolina League MVP honors; and in 1987, I was voted MVP of the Texas League. Over the three years, I hit .358. To top it off, years later, after my major league career had started, I was named Minor League Player of the Decade in the 1980s by *Baseball America*. With those minor league accolades, I felt that if I weren't the next Wade Boggs, I'd be a flop. At times, I've looked like Boggs, most notably the two years I played for the Cardinals in 1993 and 1994 when I hit .342 (and added an un-Boggs-like 46 steals) and .325. Other than those two years, hitting in the .280s and .290s with 10 home runs and 12 steals has been the norm for me. My production may have suffered over the years as a result of all the moving around from position to position as well as the bouncing around from team to team that I've done. Through 1999, I've been a starter at four different defensive positions as well as designated hitter and have suited up for six teams. Who am I?

159. Who sang the best National Anthem that Mitch ever heard? Whitney Houston? Guess again. Luther Vandross? No way. How about me? There you go. I never cut a record, but I liked to air my vocal cords in my spare time. Once, before a Cubs

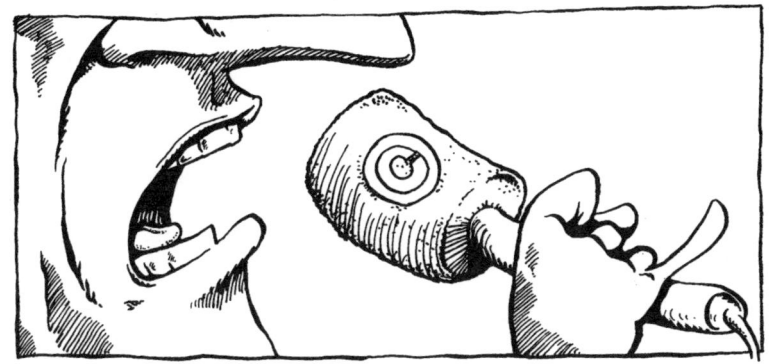

game, I had the honor of singing the National Anthem, and Mitch, along with my teammates, was duly impressed. I could play some ball, too. On the strength of a .324 average, I finished second to fellow Cub outfielder Jerome Walton in the 1989 National League Rookie of the Year vote. I didn't hit that high again, although I batted .300 on the nose for the Cubs in 1993, my last year in Chicago, and added a career-high 11 home runs. I liked playing for the Cubs, but my biggest thrill was being a part of the 1995 World Champion Braves team. Here's an oddity about my career: I could really motor in the minors—I won two stolen base titles (with Pikeville of the Appalachian League in 1984 and Pittsfield of the Eastern League in 1987) and stole 207 bases over five years, yet only stole 42 bases in my eight-year major league career. All that singing must have slowed me down. Who am I?

160. Among the guys that Mitch played with, nobody played harder for nine innings than I did. And nobody had my arm. Nobody. That shotgun arm of mine at shortstop is one of the main reasons the Cubs snapped me up first in the June 1982 draft out of Thomas Jefferson High School in Brooklyn and paid me about $150,000—which was a bundle back then. As number-one picks in the country go, my career has been in the middle of the pack—better than that of Al Chambers (Mariners in 1979) and Shawn Abner (Mets in 1984), but not as good as the career of Darryl Strawberry (Mets in 1980) or Ken Griffey Jr. (Mariners in 1987). In addition to playing a stellar short, I've had some pop in my bat; I've poked 10 homers in a season six times with a high of 17. I got my name etched in the record books when I smacked three triples in a game in 1990. Mitch used to kid me about what a free swinger I was—"Thou shall not pass," he'd say. Big Mac practically walked as many times in 1998 (162) as I did my first 15 years in the majors (192). Who am I?

161. Some people described me as a small player (I was five-foot-nine, 160 pounds) who wouldn't let bigger players intimidate me. Mitch put it more bluntly: I had a Napoleon complex. I preferred to think of myself as a scrappy, competitive player who didn't take any guff from guys that were bigger than I was. If some pitcher had a fastball that couldn't break a pane of glass, I didn't hesitate to let him know it. Case in point: There was this time when I was with the Phillies in the early 1990s, and Mark Portugal was pitching for the Astros. He was lucky enough to get me to pop up this one at bat, and on the way back to the dugout I made a wisecrack to him, and a bench-clearing brawl broke out. I was pleased with myself to cause all that commotion. I wasn't all talk, either—I could play. I was a .275 lifetime hitter, which is nothing to sneeze at for a second baseman. For the 1986 Mets, I hit .320, sharing second with Tim Teufel. In a game for the Pirates in 1990, I banged out six hits; Pete Rose never did that. After all that intensity from February to October playing baseball, insulting pitchers, and getting in fights, I spent my off-seasons relaxing on my charter fishing boat in Hawaii. Who am I?

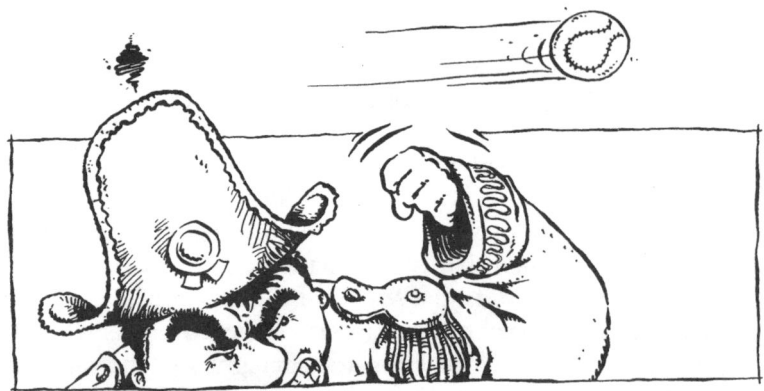

162. Oh, how I loved pizza. I would devour a few slices of pepperoni before a game, after a game, and sometimes, if my stomach was growling enough, *during* a game. When I was a reliever with the Phillies, I usually spent the first six innings in the clubhouse with Mitch and the boys before going down to the bullpen. I was known to order a pizza in the second inning, which would usually hold me over—at least until the sixth. No wonder I weighed 240 pounds. Like many players on the Phillies in 1993, I had the best season of my career that year. I led major league left-handers in games pitched with 76, posted a 2.92 ERA, and struck out 87 batters in 86⅓ innings. I started my career with the Mets, but was traded to the Twins with four other pitchers for Frank Viola in 1989. I pitched in the post-season for the 1991 Twins as well as the 1993 Phillies, but had my problems: In 9⅓ innings, my ERA was a sky-high 10.61. Who am I?

163. I was one of the best closers in baseball for a five-year period when I broke into the majors. With a deadly curveball, I was named American League Rookie of the Year in 1989 as I saved 27, punched out 90 batters in 85 innings, and finished with a flashy 1.69 ERA. Over the five years 1989–93, I saved

160 games, third among major league relievers during that time behind Eck and Big Lee Smith. By the way, some hard-throwing left-hander named Williams was tied for sixth over those five years with 154 saves. After the 1993 season, I ran into tough times. An elbow injury started my problems, and from 1994 to 1997 I pitched for six major league teams, including the Braves, Tigers, and Twins, and saved just 13 games. I hung in there, though, and my perseverance was rewarded—in 1998, I finally regained my old form: I saved 30 for the Diamondbacks. I slipped a little in 1999, but still chalked up 14 saves. Who am I?

164. I'm the pride of a small town in south-central Pennsylvania called Mount Holly Springs. As you enter the town, a sign announces that I hail from there. I made the folks back home proud by playing 12 years in the majors and hitting 90 home runs, but I wasn't at my best in the 1991 World Series for the Braves against the Twins. I hit .125 with no RBIs in 24 at bats and stranded 16 runners in scoring position. Seeing that we lost the Series in seven games and three of the four losses were by one run, I wonder if we could have won if I had delivered a couple clutch hits. Unfortunately, 1992 was almost an instant replay. I hit .200 without an RBI in 15 at bats, and we lost the Series to the Blue Jays in six games; all four losses were by one run. The next year, when the Braves picked up Fred McGriff from the Padres in July, I lost my starting first base job. A tall, strapping left-handed hitter, I played for three other National League teams besides the Braves, including the Astros in 1994, Mitch's final year in the National League and my final year in the majors. Who am I?

165. I was Mitch's teammate on two different teams: the 1989 Cubs and 1995 Angels. If you combined Mitch's velocity with my location—I walked just 2.2 batters per nine innings in my career—you would have had a dominating pitcher. I relied on my control and guile to win 163 games over a career that spanned almost two decades. I had standout years for the Expos in 1980 when I won 16 and for the A's in 1990 when I won 17, but my stuff may have been at its best for the Yankees in 1991, the year I received my first and only selection to the All-Star Game. In pinstripes that year, I won 16, which included a combined one-hit shutout against the Tigers in my first start of the year, and a one-hit shutout by myself against the Angels in July. My control was never better that year—I walked 29 batters in 208 innings. Who am I?

166. I played with guys who could outhit, outfield, and outrun me, but none of them could outdance or outshop me. I didn't have to be in a nightclub to cut up the rug; once in a while, to the amusement of my teammates, I'd start bogeying in the clubhouse. And while they would spend their afternoons on the road lounging by the hotel pool or out on the golf course, I'd be out buying up the fanciest threads money could buy. All my dancing and shopping must have created a winning atmosphere, because just about everywhere I played, we won: The 1990 Reds and 1996 Yankees won the World Series, and the 1993 Phillies made it to the World Series and lost. I was as versatile as they come—I played more than 500 games at both second base and shortstop, another 100 in the outfield, and a bunch more at first base and third base. Who am I?

167. August 4, 1982, was a fairly eventful day for me: I got hits for two different teams, in two different cities, against two pitchers who later made the Hall of Fame. Here's the way it unfolded: I played a day game for the Mets in Chicago and knocked in the winning run with a hit off Ferguson Jenkins. After the game, I learned that the Mets had traded me to the Expos, so I hopped on a plane to Philadelphia in time to get in a night game against the Phillies and collect a pinch-single off Steve Carlton. I lasted 14 years in the majors, and I was jack of all positions, master of none—especially third base. At the hot corner for the Giants in 1984, I booted 36 and fielded .887, one of the lowest marks for a regular at any position this century. I began my career in Cincinnati in 1976 and returned there to finish it in 1989. Who am I?

168. What a roller-coaster ride my career has been. It started out shakily: I went 2–10 with a 5.96 ERA for the A's in 1979, and didn't get much better the next few years (I lost a league-leading 17 for the Mariners in 1986, and six of seven decisions for the 1988 Orioles, who dropped their first 21 games and finished with a 54–107 record). And then finally, in 1989, after ten years of floundering, I found my niche with the Dodgers by ripping off three straight solid years, prompting the Cubs to sign me to a lucrative four-year contract after the 1991 season. For the Cubs in 1992, I set my career high in wins with 16, but by 1994 it was like old times as National League hitters knocked me around to the tune of a 2–10 record and 6.69 ERA. After trips to St. Louis, Cincinnati, and the minor leagues, I found myself back with the Cubs in 1998. It was there, after almost 20 years in the majors, that I did something for which fans will probably remember me most: I allowed McGwire's record-tying 61st home run. Who am I?

169. I witnessed the first pitch that Mitch threw in a major league uniform—and a strike it was not. It was spring training 1985, and Mitch had just come over to the Rangers from the Padres organization in the Rule 5 draft. Manager Doug Rader had Mitch throw some batting practice and his first pitch hit Alan Bannister in the ankle. I was standing outside the batting cage waiting to hit and decided—especially since I was a lefty—that I'd

rather not dig in against "The Wild Thing." The next day, Mitch was back on the mound throwing some more b.p., and I offered some advice to Larry Parrish as he was getting ready to hit: "Larry, as soon as he goes into his windup, you need to jump on the plate because he'll never hit you there." I held down the Rangers first base job for six years. I had a good eye at the plate, displayed a slick glove at first, and collected at least 80 RBIs in four of those years. Frustrated by back-to-back sixth-place finishes in 1987 and 1988, the Rangers cleaned house in the off-season, sending Mitch and five other players to the Cubs, and then the next day trading Oddibe McDowell, Jerry Browne, and me to the Indians for Julio Franco. I played a year with the Tribe and four more with the Mariners before I called it quits. Who am I?

170. I turned in memorable single-season performances for the California Angels, Florida Marlins, and last but certainly not least, Howard's Furniture softball team. My father and I were playing for Howard and the rest of the boys in 1984, when the Angels signed me following a tryout camp. By 1985, I was playing minor league ball; by 1987, I was pitching for the Angels; by 1989, I was saving 25 games for them; and by 1991, I was saving 46 for the Angels to lead the American League, to go along with a glittering 1.60 ERA. My great year didn't keep the Angels out of last place. An elbow injury forced me to miss most of the 1992 season, and when the Angels left me unprotected in the expansion draft, the Marlins took a gamble and snapped me up. It paid off—at least in the short term—as I nearly duplicated my 1991 season in 1993 by saving 45 with an ERA of 1.70; again, my team did not fare well, finishing in sixth place. I'm afraid to say that was my last hurrah—my elbow woes recurred in 1994, and I would save just six more games in my career. Who am I?

Mixed Bag

171. High atop the list of players with the longest hitting streaks are a few of the best hitters ever to carry lumber up to home plate. Joltin' Joe DiMaggio of course holds the record with 56 in a row, Pete Rose is tied for the National League record with 44 (Wee Willie Keeler also hit in 44 straight in 1897), Ty Cobb had streaks of 35 and 40, and Paul Molitor electrified Milwaukee with a 39-game streak in 1987. There are some other players, while regarded as good hitters, who were not in the same company as the superb stickers whom we've named, yet they compiled streaks of 25 games or longer. You would think that a player who hits in 25 straight would be on his way to a .300 season, but none of these four hit .300 in their streaky seasons. Three out of four right on this one and you can take a bow.

A. This Cubs second baseman, who played alongside Don Kessinger for years, put together streaks of 27 in 1968 and 26 in 1973. He failed to hit .300 in either season (he finished at .294 and .255 those two years) and had just one .300 season in his career.

B. His career average was an ordinary .260, and .290 was his high mark for a season in his nine-year career. But for the Braves in 1976, this left-handed hitting outfielder caught fire by hitting in 29 straight games; he finished the season at .281.

C. Also a left-handed hitting outfielder with a modest lifetime average (.268), he hit safely in 31 consecutive games for the Twins in 1980. He, too, ended the season at .281.

D. Slow journeyman catchers usually aren't candidates for long hitting streaks, but this guy rolled up a 25-game streak in 1990 for the Twins. Although he had four .300 seasons, 1990 was not one of them; he hit .294. He started with the Angels in 1979 and wrapped up with the A's in 1995.

172. It's amazing how the Dodgers have churned out so many Rookies of the Year. Starting with Jackie Robinson in 1947, the year the award was instituted, 16 Dodgers have been named the National League's best rookie. In a recent 18-year stretch (1979–96), no less than *nine* players who wore Dodger blue won the honor. One began his rookie campaign 8–0 with five shutouts; one winner finished his career in 1994 with almost 2000 hits; one played for three teams in one week in May 1998; one captured an ERA title for the Indians; one was suspended more times than Albert Belle; the lone first baseman in the group has rattled off a number of 30–home run, 100-RBI seasons; one winner hails from the Dominican Republic and is a great defensive outfielder; one Rookie of the Year tossed a no-hitter in his sophomore season against the hard-hitting Rockies; and the most recent recipient of the award won with rather modest numbers: a .291 average, 12 home runs, and 59 RBIs. How many of these nine freshmen Dodger standouts can you come up with?

173. Over in the American League, no team has dominated the Rookie of the Year Award like the Dodgers. The Yankees have had eight winners, and five other teams have turned out five or more winners. Match these junior circuit Rookies of the Year with the facts we've given.

Ron Hansen **A.** Hit 35 home runs for the White Sox in 1983 to win award
Ron Kittle **B.** Won award for Orioles; later pulled off an unassisted triple play, hit a grand slam, and was traded—in the same week
Tim Salmon **C.** Only player to win Rookie of the Year and MVP the same season
Fred Lynn **D.** Won award unanimously in 1972
Carlton Fisk **E.** Only Angel through 1999 to win award

174. There are a few things we all know about Cal Ripken Jr.: He's been a fixture in the Orioles infield since 1982; he broke Lou Gehrig's consecutive games record in 1995; and he'll be elected to the Hall of Fame the first year that he's eligible. Here are four more facts about the Oriole superstar, along with one statement about Cal that's not true. Which one is it?

A. He was named MVP of an All-Star Game.
B. He won the American League Rookie of the Year Award.
C. He holds the major league record for fewest errors in a season by a shortstop.
D. He was named MVP of the American League twice.
E. He led the major league in home runs one season.

175. You'd be hard-pressed to name a pair of brothers whose careers were more similar than this duo's. Both were right-handers who stood six-four and weighed between 200 and 210 pounds. Both pitched 16 years in the majors; the older brother broke in with the Astros, while the younger brother finished up with the Astros. The older brother pitched 70 career complete games and 18 shutouts, while his younger brother completed 67 games and tossed 19 shutouts. The younger brother threw two no-hitters—in 1978 and 1983—while the older brother threw one in 1979. Name these brothers.

176. You'll always think of Hank Aaron as a Brave, Willie Mays as a Giant, and Billy Williams as a Cub, but these greats, as well as some others, did not finish their careers with the same teams for whom they starred. Match these five players with their final big league clubs.

Billy Williams   **A.** Oakland A's
Dale Murphy   **B.** Cleveland Indians
Willie Mays   **C.** Milwaukee Brewers
Keith Hernandez   **D.** Colorado Rockies
Hank Aaron   **E.** New York Mets

177. Managers always incite their players to take spring training seriously, so when the season starts, they're ready to grab a foothold on first place. As two teams—one in each league—proved in the 1980s, a terrific start doesn't guarantee a pennant. Both teams opened the season unbeatable, winning their first 13 games, only to play mediocre ball the remainder of the year. The National League team went 76–73 the rest of the way and barely hung on to win the division. They were quickly eliminated in the playoffs by losing three straight. Claudell Washington led this quick-starting team that faded fast, with 33 stolen bases; wily veteran Gene Garber headed the bullpen with 30 saves; and Jerry Royster did an admirable job as a role player. In manager Tom Trebelhorn's first full year, the American League team fizzled after their red-hot start and finished in third place, seven games out, with a 91–71 record. Rob Deer paced Trebelhorn's club with 28 home runs, and Teddy Higuera, a promising pitcher whose career was cut short because of arm problems, won 18 games. Name these teams who are etched in the record books for their early-season winning streaks, and the years they set their marks.

178. Dykstra, Daulton, and Mitch got a lot of the headlines for the '93 Phillies, but it was a team effort to win the division and beat the Braves in the playoffs. There were many guys on the Philadelphia team who made valuable contributions but didn't get much ink. Here are brief descriptions of five of those players. You Phillies fans will rattle these off quicker than you can say Steve Jeltz. The rest of you will have to labor to remember three of these unsung players.

   A. This pitcher from North Carolina tied Curt Schilling for most wins during the regular season with 16; two years earlier, he no-hit the Expos.
   B. The Phillies brought up this player from the minors mid-season to take over the shortstop job, and he responded by hitting .324.
   C. He backed up John Kruk capably at first base and was a good pinch-hitter.
   D. Tourette's syndrome kept him out of baseball for two full years and parts of three others in his 20s. He learned to control the disorder and became a steady .300 hitter and fan favorite in Philadelphia; he hit .318 in '93.
   E. This was his second tour of duty with the Phillies; he played with the Cardinals for four years in between. For the '93 Phillies he platooned in the outfield and batted .262.

179. When Ozzie Smith's name pops into your head, you probably picture him making an incredible play at shortstop for the Cardinals. And Amos Otis spent so many years gobbling up fly balls in the Royals outfield, you may assume that he played his entire career in Kansas City. Actually, both Ozzie and Amos, as well as three other players we've listed below, started their careers for teams different from whom they had their best years. See if you can match these players with their first major league teams.

   Ryne Sandberg   **A.** Philadelphia Phillies
   Lou Brock   **B.** Minnesota Twins
   Amos Otis   **C.** New York Mets
   Ozzie Smith   **D.** Chicago Cubs
   Graig Nettles   **E.** San Diego Padres

180. Since their inaugural year in 1969, the Expos have had many outstanding players including Andre Dawson, Gary Carter, and Vladimir Guerrero, yet the team has not been to the World Series, and no Expo has ever won the MVP or led the league in home runs. Two Expos, however, have won batting titles, and one has captured the Cy Young Award. The first Expo batting titlist led the loop in 1982 with a .331 average; it was one of only two years he spent in Montreal in a career that spanned 18 years during which he accumulated more than 2700 hits. The second topped the National League in 1986 with a .334 mark; he delivered his 2500th hit in 1998 for an American League team. The Expo who won the Cy Young Award did so recently, but departed after the season to sign as a free agent with another team for whom he has since won another Cy Young. Name these excellent Expos.

181. In the music world they are referred to as "one-hit wonders": artists who turn out one big hit and then fade into obscurity. In the baseball world they are called "one-season wonders": players with otherwise undistinguished careers, who for one shining season play like All-Stars. Here are descriptions of four players in that category.
   A. Indians fans probably would have voted him mayor after he hit .289 with 23 home runs and 87 RBIs to win the 1980 American League Rookie of the Year Award. He was so popular in Cleveland that a song was named after him. His success was short-lived, though, as he hit .211 over the next two years and vanished from baseball.
   B. For the Marlins in 1993 this Cuban first baseman hit 20 home runs with 87 RBIs. In the rest of his major league career he hit six home runs with 19 RBIs.
   C. He pitched seven years in the majors. In six of those years, his combined record was 15–29 with a 4.94 ERA. But in one outstanding season for the Braves (1974), he mastered National League hitters—he was 16–8 with a league-leading 2.28 ERA.
   D. This right-hander pitched 10 years in the majors for the A's and compiled a career record of 58–59. Typical seasons were 4–5, 5–8, and 7–11. But in 1980, he finished second in the Cy Young vote with a 22–9 record, 2.54 ERA, and 24 complete games.

182. There's nothing in baseball quite like a neck-and-neck pennant race that goes down to the wire. Since divisional play began in 1969, many division races have been unsettled until the last day of the season; some have required a one-game playoff because two teams finished the regular season tied. See if you can remember these teams, which either prevailed or succumbed under the pressure in a big game to decide the division.

  A. They were in first place by 14 games on July 17, 1978, but the second-place team clawed back the last two and a half months of the season, and the teams finished in a dead heat. The collapse became complete when they lost a one-game playoff 5–4; Bucky Dent's three-run homer was the big blow. What team squandered the big lead?

  B. The Champagne corks were flying when the Mariners earned their first trip to the post-season by beating this team in a one-game showdown for the American League Western Division Championship in 1995.

  C. Having announced his retirement effective the end of the 1982 season, Orioles manager Earl Weaver was eager to return to the World Series one last time. His Birds trailed the first-place team by three games and squared off against them in a four-game series the last weekend of the season at the old Baltimore Memorial Stadium. The Orioles won the first three games to draw even, and then disappointed a maddening Orioles crowd by losing 10–2 on the last day of the season. Name the team that denied Earl the opportunity to advance to the playoffs.

  D. Three teams were in contention for the National League wild-card berth the last week of the 1998 season. Whom did the Cubs beat in a one-game playoff to move on and play the Braves in the Division Series?

183. It's one of baseball's toughest jobs: sitting on the bench for eight innings and then getting called on to pinch-hit in the ninth with the tying run on third base against some reliever throwing 95-mile-an-hour bullets. Some players have handled this role exceptionally well. See if you can identify these pinch-hitters extraordinaire.

A. This burly catcher/first baseman who never shied away from a fight, smacked a record 20 pinch-hit homers in his career that began with the Astros in 1972 and ended with the Blue Jays in 1986.

B. He was well suited for the job: He couldn't run or play defense particularly well, but he had a good eye at the plate and a nice compact stroke that produced many a line drive. He holds the all-time record for career pinch-hits with 150, which included 10 or more in a season twice for the Pirates in the 1960s and seven times for the Dodgers in the 1970s.

C. Fans were scratching their heads when Padres manager Bruce Bochy sent this player out to pinch-*run* in the bottom of the ninth inning of Game 3 of the 1998 World Series instead of pinch-hit. After all, he had set the major league record by collecting 28 pinch-hits for the Rockies in 1995.

D. In an amazing 11-day stretch in 1979, this reserve Phillies outfielder tied a record by homering in three consecutive at bats as a pinch-hitter.

184. Let's move from pinch-hitters to pinch-runners. In 1974, the A's signed a world-class sprinter with no professional baseball experience as the game's first—and only—full-time pinch-runner. Without ever batting or playing the field, he made 91 pinch-running appearances, stealing 28 bases and scoring 29 runs. He was used in a similar role the next year for 13 games, before the A's released him. From 1975 to 1977, the A's used another player primarily as a pinch-runner, although he was a baseball player by trade—the Cubs drafted him in 1968, and he played four years in the minors as an infielder/outfielder. During his three years with the A's, this speedster collected just 12 hits in 82 at bats, but scored 56 runs and stole 63 bases. The Pirates used him in the same way from 1978 to 1981. Over those four years, he only had 27 at bats (and he got 12 hits for a .444 average), but he scored 36 runs and stole 30 bases. No players since have been used to that extent as pinch-runners. We'll be impressed if you can remember either one; drinks are on Mitch if you rattle off both.

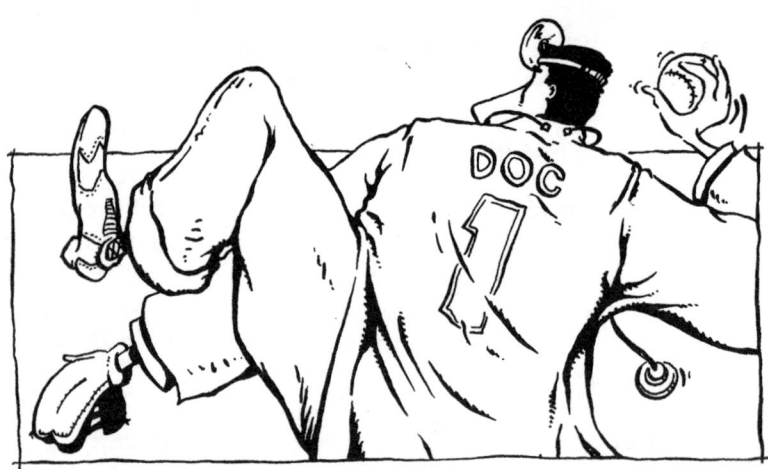

185. Unlike basketball and football players who are predominantly drafted out of college, many baseball players sign out of high school and forgo college to start playing in the minors. There have been a few players, and at least one manager, who not only went to college, they attended academic powerhouses or obtained advanced degrees. Can you name...

    A. the pitcher who won 124 games in the '70s and early '80s, nicknamed "Doc" because he graduated from the University of Pittsburgh's medical school during his playing career?

    B. the manager, who was at the helm of a big league team in 1999, who received his law degree from Florida State University in 1980?

    C. the heady hurler, who pitched mostly for the Mets and A's, that went to Yale University?

    D. the outfielder, who collected 204 hits in 1999, that earned a degree in systems science and engineering from the University of Pennsylvania?

186. The 1990s are behind us, and if we asked you to name teams that had winning records over the decade, we'd expect to hear you belt out the Indians and the Braves in short order. And if we asked for teams in the '90s that failed to win a post-season game, we suspect the Royals and the Tigers might be some of your early guesses. Here's a twist: There were two teams that had winning records over those 10 years and did not celebrate a single post-season victory. Let's hear them.

187. Baseball doesn't have the bone-crushing hits that football has, but the game is not without its injuries. Some of the more serious ones are sustained when a batter is hit by a pitch or a pitcher gets nailed by a line drive. Here are questions about four such victims; these injuries virtually ended all of their careers, and three of the four were victimized when they were 27 or younger.

A. Your father or grandfather will remember in a second this great catcher for the Philadelphia A's and Tigers in the 1920s and 1930s. He hit .330 five times, and one year struck out just eight times in 514 at bats. But his career ended abruptly in May 1937 when he was hit in the head with a pitch.

B. Two months later, in July 1937, this Cardinals right-hander was on the top of the world: He was starting the All-Star Game, and although he was only 26, had already won 134 games. In a 1934 double-header, he threw a two-hit shutout in the opener, and his brother threw a no-hitter in the second game, prompting him to joke, "If I'd known he was going to throw a no-hitter, I would've thrown one myself." But his career went downhill quickly when Earl Averill hit him in the toe with a line drive in the 1937 All-Star Game. He tried to come back too soon, which messed up his motion, and he hurt his arm. He retired when he was 30.

C. The Indians thought they had another Bob Feller when this lefty won 36 games and led the American League in strikeouts his first two seasons in 1955 and 1956. But then, in 1957, Yankees shortstop Gil McDougald hit him in the eye with a line drive, and he was never the same again. He won 17 more games and was out of baseball when he was 28.

D. This guy might have hit 600 home runs if it weren't for a fastball he took in the eye in 1967. He was 22 and had already hit 100 home runs. The injury sidelined him for a year and a half, and even though he made a valiant comeback by hitting 20 and 36 home runs in 1969 and 1970, his vision problems recurred, and he hit just six more home runs.

188. Since the institution of the World Series MVP Award in 1955, only one player has won the award for a team that lost the Series. Game 1, his team lost 6–4, and he went hitless. His team bounced back to win big in Game 2, 16–3, and he contributed three hits and two RBIs. His bat got hotter in Game 3, as he connected for a grand slam and added a two-run single to lead his club to a 10–0 victory. It was back to earth for this player in Games 4 and 5; his team lost 3–2 and 5–2, and he went 2 for 7 with one RBI. His team evened the Series at three by slaughtering their opponent, 12–0, in Game 6; the eventual Series MVP had two triples and three RBIs. He went 2 for 5 in Game 7 without an RBI, as his team dropped a cliffhanger 10–9 to lose the Series 4–3. All told, he hit .367 and set a World Series record that hasn't been matched with 12 RBIs. Funny thing is, he was no slugger; he never drove in more than 59 runs in a season in his 12-year career, and in the year of his great Series, he collected just 26 RBIs in 460 at bats during the regular season. Name the player and the year of the Series.

189. Sit back for a minute and remember the careers of these front-line starting pitchers: Ken Holtzman, Joaquin Andujar, Jack Morris, and Frank Viola. Listed below are five statements. Every one is true with regard to at least two of the pitchers, but only one is, with regard to all four. Which one is it?

A. He won the seventh game of a World Series.
B. He pitched a no-hitter.
C. He finished his major league career with the same team with which he began it.
D. He never pitched for the Red Sox, White Sox, or Yankees.
E. He won and lost at least 150 regular season games.

190. Including reserves, Mitch pitched to more than 15 catchers in his career. Match these backstops with the teams for whom they caught Mitch.

Jorge Fabregas   **A.** Texas Rangers
Todd Pratt   **B.** Chicago Cubs
Geno Petralli   **C.** Philadelphia Phillies
Rick Wrona   **D.** Houston Astros
Scott Servais   **E.** California Angels

191. We agree that sometimes when a team is having a rough year, the owner or general manager has to shake things up by changing managers. But let's not get carried away. There was a team who changed managers 13 consecutive years. Most of the skippers were fired by the team's ornery owner; some resigned. Managers who got canned by this owner included Harry Craft, Ed Lopat, and Alvin Dark. Name the owner who changed managers at the drop of a hat.

    A. Marge Schott
    B. George Steinbrenner
    C. Charley Finley
    D. Clark Griffith
    E. Bill Veeck

192. Mitch was thrilled when Tommy Lasorda named him to the National League All-Star squad in 1989. Mitch got into the game and pitched a scoreless inning, walking one and striking out one. While some fans moan and groan that the All-Star Game sometimes doesn't live up to its hype, there have been some memorable moments in the Mid-season Classic. Here are five—do your best to tell us what year they happened. If you come within a year, that's close enough.

    A. Twenty-one-year-old phenom Vida Blue had the honor of starting for the American League, and the first batter he faced was his boyhood idol, 40-year-old Willie Mays.
    B. Fred Lynn capped a seven-run third inning for the American League by hitting the first grand slam in All-Star Game history.
    C. In the longest All-Star Game to date, Tony Perez won it for the National League with a home run off Catfish Hunter in the top of the 15th inning.
    D. Providing National League fans with more ammunition that their league was superior, Dave Concepcion hit a two-run homer and starter Steve Rogers pitched three strong innings to lead the senior circuit to its 19th win in 20 games.
    E. The Marlins' Jeff Conine was named MVP of the game by delivering a key pinch-hit home run in the eighth inning, which proved to be the game-winner.

193. Why is it that left-handed pitchers are often nicknamed "Lefty" but right-handers are never nicknamed "Righty"? The "Leftys" have included some of the game's best ever as well as a guy who was banned from baseball for his participation in the Black Sox scandal. Match these pitchers nicknamed "Lefty" with the brief descriptions of their careers that we've given you.

Lefty Grove   **A.** Steady pitcher for the Pirates early in the century; won 15 or more for six straight years

Lefty Gomez   **B.** Undistinguished career for pre–World War II St. Louis Browns

Lefty Leifield   **C.** Hall-of-Famer who won 300 games for the A's and Red Sox

Lefty Williams   **D.** Hall-of-Famer who won 20 games four times for the Yankees

Lefty Mills   **E.** Won 23 games for the White Sox in 1919, but then accepted money from gamblers to throw the World Series

194. Since the Boston Pilgrims and Pittsburgh Pirates knocked heads in 1903, there have been 96 World Series, yet only a handful of players have homered for an American League team and a National League team in the Series? One active player has accomplished this feat. Try to pick him out from these five players and, for extra credit, give us the years and teams.

   A. Jim Leyritz
   B. Matt Williams
   C. Paul O'Neill
   D. David Justice
   E. Bobby Bonilla

195. Two relievers, a left-hander and right-hander, each at the end of the line and who earlier in their career put together a sensational year out of the bullpen, spent part of the 1993 season with Mitch's Phillies. The lefty won the Cy Young Award for the Padres in 1989 with 44 saves and a 1.85 ERA. He signed a lucrative contract with the Royals after his big season, but got roughed up in his two and a half years in Kansas City. The Phillies, for whom he started his career in 1980, acquired him from the Braves in April 1993 and he pitched in 25 games before they released him in July. Five weeks later, the Phillies signed a right-hander who three years earlier had set the all-time single-season save record by saving 57 games for the White Sox. His pitching fell off after his record-breaking year, and finally the Chisox traded him to the Phillies in August 1993. He appeared in 17 games the final seven weeks of the season and pitched in the post-season against the Braves and Blue Jays. Name these pitchers.

196. To win a league MVP, a player has to put together some very good stats over a 162-game season. But to be named MVP of a World Series, he only needs to get hot for a few games. Don Larsen (1956), Bucky Dent (1978), and Rick Dempsey (1983) each won World Series MVPs, but they didn't come close to winning a league MVP. Let's see how well you know your league and World Series MVP winners. Which of the following statements is *not* true?
- **A.** Orel Hershiser won a World Series MVP, but did not win a league MVP.
- **B.** George Foster did not win a World Series MVP, but did win a league MVP.
- **C.** Brooks Robinson won a World Series MVP and a league MVP.
- **D.** Gary Carter won a World Series MVP, but did not win a league MVP.
- **E.** Sal Bando did not win a World Series MVP, nor did he win a league MVP.

197. Which of these two major league records did Mitch set in his career? (The first one has since been broken.)
- **A.** Most saves by a rookie reliever in a month and most consecutive strikeouts by a left-handed pitcher
- **B.** Most innings by a left-handed reliever in a season not allowing a home run and most consecutive appearances by a pitcher without starting a game
- **C.** Most strikeouts by a left-handed rookie reliever in a season and most consecutive save opportunities converted
- **D.** Most walks issued by a reliever in a month and most consecutive appearances without allowing an earned run
- **E.** Most games pitched by a rookie in a season and most wins by a reliever in a month

198. When Billy Martin was growing up in Oakland, his mother urged him not to take any nonsense from anybody. As George Steinbrenner can attest to, Billy took Mom's advice. Unfortunately for Billy, George's mother must have had the same motto—her son fired Billy five times, but Martin, who coveted the job as Yankees manager, kept coming back. You associate Billy so much with the Yankees that it's easy to forget he managed four other American League teams, three before he ever got the Yankees job and one between his second and third stints as Yankees skipper. He won divisions for three of those teams and finished second for the other after they had lost 105 games the year before. Name the four teams besides the Yankees that Alfred Manuel "Billy" Martin managed.

199. Dating back to their early days in cozy Ebbets Field, the Dodgers have turned out more than their share of sluggers, such as Gil Hodges, Roy Campanella, and Ron Cey, but none is their all-time home run leader. Who is? The Astros, on the other hand, have a long line of fast players who legged out a lot of triples. Joe Morgan, Cesar Cedeno, and Terry Puhl all hit more than 50 triples for the Astros, but somebody else hit more. Can you hazard a guess who? In addition to these two, we've listed eight teams and asked you to identify their all-time leader in a certain hit category.

Team	Category
A. California/Anaheim Angels	Doubles
B. Chicago White Sox	Home runs
C. Milwaukee Brewers	Singles
D. New York Yankees	Triples
E. Toronto Blue Jays	Doubles
F. Houston Colt 45's/Astros	Triples
G. Brooklyn/Los Angeles Dodgers	Home runs
H. Montreal Expos	Doubles
I. New York Mets	Triples
J. Philadelphia Phillies	Singles

200. When you look at this team's numbers for the year, you will not be impressed. They stole the grand total of 27 bases, and their team leader had six. In the 12-team league, they ranked

11th in batting average and runs scored. No player scored more than 85 runs, and only two hitters tallied more than 60 RBIs. They finished 11th in doubles, 10th in triples, and 11th in home runs. Their pitching was good, but still only one pitcher won more than 14 games. In fact, on the morning of August 17, they were in dead last in their division, seven and a half games out of first. But in the last seven weeks, they caught fire, passing all five teams and eking out the division title with a .509 percentage. In a hard-fought Championship Series, which included some fisticuffs, they prevailed, three games to two. This Cinderella team almost won the whole ball of wax, as they took a 3–2 lead in the World Series only to drop the last two. Can you identify these overachievers (team and year, please) whose roster included the likes of George Stone, George Theodore, and Don Hahn?

Answers

HANGING CURVEBALLS

Who Am I?
1. Mark McGwire
2. Jose Canseco
3. George Brett
4. Bobby Bonds
5. Kirby Puckett
6. Barry Larkin
7. Dwight Gooden
8. Don Drysdale
9. Deion Sanders
10. Will "The Thrill" Clark
11. Dave Winfield
12. Curt Flood
13. Wade Boggs
14. Ozzie Smith
15. Jeff Bagwell
16. Tony Perez
17. Dennis Martinez
18. Mike Piazza
19. Lee Smith
20. Bert Blyleven

Mixed Bag
21. Mike Schmidt (Phillies), Mickey Mantle (Yankees), Ted Williams (Red Sox), Ernie Banks (Cubs), and Mel Ott (Giants)
22. 46 (43 in the regular season, two in the League Championship Series, and one in the World Series)
23. Indians—A (Lost 1995 and 1997 Series)
    Twins—E (Won 1987 and 1991 Series)
    Padres—D (Lost 1984 and 1998 Series)
    Mets—C (Won 1986 Series)
    Reds—B (Won 1990 Series)
24. **A.** Ron Cey
    B. Dave Parker
    C. Mark Fidrych
    D. Andre Dawson
    E. Orel Hershiser
25. Billy Williams and Steve Garvey
26. A. Cepeda won the N.L. MVP in 1967; Yount won the A.L.

MVP in 1982 and 1989; Rice won the A.L. MVP in 1978; and McCovey won the N.L. MVP in 1969. Murray never won one, but he received more overall votes than any American League player in the 1980s.

27. Pitcher—Jim Kaat
Catcher—Johnny Bench
First base—Keith Hernandez
Second base—Ryne Sandberg
Shortstop—Ozzie Smith
Third base—Brooks Robinson
Outfield (Pirates)—Roberto Clemente
Outfield (Giants)—Willie Mays
Outfield (Tigers)—Al Kaline
Outfield (Mariners)—Ken Griffey Jr.

28. A. True. He stole a surprising 123 bases.
  B. True. He played one year for the Braves, in 1935.
  C. False. It was the other way around.
  D. True. He won 23 in 1916 and 24 in 1917.
  E. True. He edged out Gehrig, .342 to .340.
  F. False. Hank Aaron beat him out, 2297 to 2212.
  G. False. Not even close—93 was his high.
  H. True.
  I. False. His high mark in a season was .393.
  J. False. That's pathetic if you missed this one.

29. Johnstone—C (with Rick Talley)
Lyle—B (co-authored by Peter Golenbock)
Bouton—D
Perry—A (with Bob Sudyk)
Pepitone—E (with Berry Stainback; full title: *Joe, You Could've Made Us Proud*)

30. Lou Whitaker (Tigers)
Ron Guidry (Yankees)
Dave Concepcion (Reds)
Scott McGregor (Orioles)
Paul Splittorff (Royals)

31. Sutter—D
McGraw—C
Wilhelm—A
Giusti—E
Face—B

32. Yogi Berra (14 as a player for the Yankees, four as a coach of the Yankees, one as a coach of the Mets, one as manager of the Yankees, and one as manager of the Mets)

33. Paul Molitor (3319 hits, 234 home runs, and 504 stolen bases) and Eddie Murray (3255 hits, 504 home runs, and 110 stolen bases)

34.

Decade	National League	American League
1950s	Dodgers (913)	Yankees (955)
1960s	Cardinals (884)	Orioles (911)
1970s	Reds (953)	Orioles (944)
1980s	Dodgers/Cardinals (825)	Yankees (854)
1990s	Braves (925)	Yankees (851)

35. Stargell—A. He was elected his first year in 1988.
Aparicio—C. He was elected his sixth year in 1984.
Campanella—C. He was elected his seventh year in 1969.
Jackson—A. He was elected his first year in 1993.
Bunning—D. He was elected by the Veterans Committee in 1996.
Palmer—A. He was elected his first year in 1990.
Killebrew—B. He was elected his fourth year in 1984.
Niekro—B. He was elected his fifth year in 1997.
Rizzuto—D. He was elected by the Veterans Committee in 1994.
Hunter—B. He was elected his third year in 1987.

36. **A.** Danny Ainge
  B. Dave DeBusschere
  C. Ron Reed
  D. Terry Francona

37. The 1976 Reds; they swept the Phillies in the League Championship Series and the Yankees in the World Series.

38. Gene Mauch

39. Stan Musial, Ken Griffey, and Ken Griffey Jr.

40. **A.** Rod Carew
  B. Don Wilson
  C. Roberto Clemente
  D. Casey Stengel
  E. Warren Spahn

41. C. Mitch moved to Oregon when he was five.

42. Howe—E
Torre—B
Alou—C
Garner—D
Johnson—A
43. Cubs—D
Cardinals—A
Dodgers—B
Phillies—E
Tigers—C
44. **A.** George Hendrick
B. Gary Matthews
C. Tony Armas
D. Richie Zisk
E. Gene Tenace
45. **A.** Ferguson Jenkins
B. Tommy John
C. Jerry Koosman
D. Joe Niekro
E. Jerry Reuss
46. Carl Yastrzemski
47. **A.** Bobby Thomson
B. Bob Lemon and Early Wynn
C. Don Larsen
D. Lew Burdette
48. Chicago White Sox
49. Boston
50. Orlando Cepeda (1961), Willie McCovey (1968–69), Will Clark (1988), Kevin Mitchell (1989), Matt Williams (1990), and Barry Bonds (1993)

CHANGE-UPS AT THE LETTERS

Who Am I?
51. Harold Baines
52. Mark Grace
53. John Kruk
54. Fred McGriff
55. Dave Stewart
56. John Franco
57. George Bell
58. Bo Jackson
59. Darrell Evans
60. Larry Walker

61. Lenny Dykstra
62. Howard Johnson
63. Kirk Gibson
64. Ivan Rodriguez
65. Ted Simmons
66. Charlie Hough
67. Frank Tanana
68. Bobby Bonilla
69. Dwight Evans
70. Jack Clark

Mixed Bag

71. Pitcher Hal Newhouser (A.L., 1944–45), catcher Yogi Berra (A.L., 1954–55), first baseman Jimmie Foxx (A.L., 1932–33), second baseman Joe Morgan (N.L., 1975–76), shortstop Ernie Banks (N.L., 1958–59), third baseman Mike Schmidt (N.L., 1980–81), and outfielders Mickey Mantle (A.L., 1956–57), Roger Maris (A.L., 1960–61), and Dale Murphy (N.L., 1982–83). Newhouser, Berra, Foxx, Morgan, Banks, Schmidt, and Mantle are in the Hall of Fame; Maris probably won't make it; and Murphy was eligible for the first time in 1999 and received 96 out of 497 votes.

72. Valentine—Yes (Rangers in 1986, 1987, and 1988)
Zimmer—Yes (Cubs in 1989 and 1990)
Fregosi—Yes (Phillies in 1991, 1992, and 1993)
Kennedy—No
Johnson—No
Riggleman—No
Oates—No
Collins—Yes (Astros in 1994)
Rodgers—No
Lachemann—Yes (Angels in 1995)

73. Brown. Gates was a reserve outfielder for the Tigers from 1963 to 1975; Ollie went downtown 20 times for the Padres in 1969 and 23 more in 1970; Kevin signed that lofty nine-figure deal for the Dodgers in December 1998; and Chris hit .294 for the Giants in 1985–86, his first two full seasons in the majors, but was out of baseball before he was 30.

74. Williams. Charlie was traded for Willie early in the 1972 season; Ted did a fairly good job of achieving his goal—he was a lifetime .344 hitter; Bernie hit .339 in 1998 to win the batting title; Walt played six (1967–72) of his 10 major league seasons with the Chisox.

75. The Tigers traded John Smoltz for Doyle Alexander.

76. Houston Astros

77. The Twins' Jack Morris beat the Braves, 1–0, in Game 7 of the 1991 World Series. The Phillies' Curt Schilling shut out the Blue Jays, 2–0, in Game 5 of the 1993 Series. And the Yankees' Andy Pettitte pitched eight and one third shutout innings against the Braves in Game 5 of the 1996 Series and held the Padres scoreless for seven and one third innings in Game 4 of the 1998 Classic.

78. A. False. The Browns didn't move to Baltimore until after the 1953 season.

B. False. It seemed like 25 years to the fans in Kansas City, but it was only 13. The A's had a losing record every year in Kansas City and never finished higher than sixth place.

C. True. The Pilots played there in 1969 before bankruptcy forced the franchise to move to Milwaukee.

D. True

E. True

79.   **A.** Michael Jackson
      B. Terry Bradshaw
      C. Kenny Rogers
      D. Gary Cooper

80.   Maddux—D
      May—A (The Brewers traded Dave May and pitcher Roger Alexander to the Braves for Aaron in November 1974.)
      Assenmacher—C
      Salazar—B
      Schiraldi—E

81. Rusty Staub

82. B

83. Rick Wise. The Phillies traded him to the Cardinals for Steve Carlton in February 1972.

84.   **A.** Nolan Ryan
      B. Bobby Witt
      C. Mike Torrez
      D. Bob Feller

85. The Dodgers' Walter Alston (1954–76) and Tommy Lasorda (1977–96)

86.   **A.** Jim Konstanty
      B. Tug McGraw
      C. Al Holland
      D. Steve Bedrosian

87. Seaver played with Jesse Orosco and Darryl Strawberry on the Mets; Harold Baines, Ozzie Guillen, Bobby Bonilla, and John Cangelosi on the White Sox; and Roger Clemens and Wade Boggs on the Red Sox. Their 1999 teams were as follows: Orosco (Orioles); Strawberry (Yankees); Baines (Orioles and Indians); Guillen (Braves); Bonilla (Mets); Cangelosi (Rockies); Clemens (Yankees); and Boggs (Devil Rays)

88. Catcher—Sandy Alomar
Second base—Carlos Baerga
Third base—Jim Thome
Left field—Albert Belle
Center field—Kenny Lofton
Right field—Manny Ramirez
Designated hitter—Eddie Murray

89. Valentine—Expos
Van Slyke—Pirates
Kennedy—Padres
Hurst—Red Sox
Boddicker—Orioles

90. A. Marichal played in the 1962 Series for the Giants; Niekro didn't play in a Series.

B. Jim played in the 1965 Series for the Twins; Gaylord didn't play in a Series.

C. Tiant played in the 1975 Series for the Red Sox; Jenkins didn't play in a Series.

D. Yount played in the 1982 Series for the Brewers; Carew didn't play in a Series.

E. Winfield played in the 1981 Series for the Yankees and the 1992 Series for the Blue Jays; Dawson didn't play in a Series.

91. Vida Blue
  A. Von Hayes
  B. Chuck Knoblauch
  C. Gary Carter

92. **A.** Clemens (5–4)
  B. Maddux (5–2)
  C. Maddux (11–3)
  D. Maddux (2.03–2.86)
  E. Clemens (5–0)
  F. Clemens (.648–.637)

    G. Maddux (10–0)
    H. Clemens (5–2)
    I. Clemens (1–0)
    J. Maddux (2.81–3.04)
It's a dead heat: five for Roger and five for Greg.
  93. George Foster (1976–78) and Cecil Fielder (1990–92)
  94. Reggie Jackson
  95. Starting left fielder—Moises Alou
      Closer—Robb Nen
      Starting center fielder—Devon White
      Starting pitcher (Padres)—Kevin Brown
      Starting pitcher (Mets)—Al Leiter
      Starting third baseman—Gary Sheffield
      Starting right fielder—Bobby Bonilla
      Starting catcher—Charles Johnson
      Reserve outfielder—Jim Eisenreich
  96. Schilling—D
      Nilsson—B
      Davis—E
      Darling—A
      Blowers—C
  97. Buddy Bell
  98. Ty Cobb—2244 runs scored, plus 1959 RBIs less 118 home runs for 4085 runs produced
  99. Chuck Tanner
100. Mariners—B
      Expos—C
      Angels—E
      Senators—A
      Blue Jays—D

SLIDERS DOWN AND IN

Who Am I?

101. Don Slaught
102. Joe Girardi
103. Larry Andersen
104. Ruben Sierra
105. John Candelaria
106. Jose Rijo
107. Jim Thome
108. Pete Incaviglia
109. Mike Maddux
110. Rob Dibble

111. Robin Ventura
112. Steve Buechele
113. Mickey Tettleton
114. Dave Hollins
115. Danny Tartabull
116. Brady Anderson
117. Kent Hrbek
118. John Tudor
119. Darrell Porter
120. Rick Sutcliffe

Mixed Bag
121. **A.** Richie Ashburn
    B. Roger Craig
    C. Frank Thomas
    D. Marv Throneberry
122. Fletcher—B
    Ward—E
    Sundberg—A
    Harrah—C
    Paciorek—D
123. 1974
124. Ryan—B
    Carlton—E
    Gibson—C
    Palmer—A
    Sutton—D
125. E. This one was a knucklecurveball. In 16 career at bats, Mitch hit one home run for a ratio of 16.00, which was better than Stargell (16.69), Banks (18.40), Bench (19.69), and Rice (21.53). Mitch says you can take credit if you guessed Stargell.
126. A
127. **A.** Joe DiMaggio
    B. Dick Allen
    C. Jose Cruz
    D. Ken Boyer
    E. Felipe Alou
128. **A.** Bob Boone
    B. Sandy Alomar
    C. Mel Stottlemyre
    D. Manny Mota
    E. Sam Hairston
129. Steve Stone won 25 for the Orioles in 1980; Bob Welch won 27 for the A's in 1990.

130. Aaron—B (328)
Ripken—C (646 in 1989)
Robinson—D
Jackson—E (2597)
Mantle—A (54)
131. C
132. Henderson—B
Wilson—A
Hernandez—D
Morgan—E
Sandberg—C
Henderson (2816 through 1999), Morgan (2517), Sandberg (2386), Wilson (2207), Hernandez (2182)
133. **A.** Babe Dahlgren
B. Carl Yastrzemski
C. Doug DeCinces
D. Rick Cerone
134. E
135. **A.** Maury Wills
B. Vince Coleman
C. Joe Morgan
D. Willie Wilson
136. B
137. C
138. D
139. **A.** Mark Belanger
B. Eddie Brinkman
C. Bud Harrleson
D. Bobby Wine
E. Hal Lanier
140. Len Barker (Indians), Mike Witt (Angels), Tom Browning (Reds), Dennis Martinez (Expos), Kenny Rogers (Rangers), David Wells (1998 Yankees), and David Cone (1999 Yankees)
141. Moffitt—D
Knight—A
LaCock—B
Justice—E
Lahti—C

142. **A.** David Cone
   B. Darryl Strawberry
   C. Dave Kingman
   D. Phil Linz
143. **A.** Dallas Green
   B. Joe Altobelli
   C. Dick Howser
   D. Cito Gaston
144. A (For the Rockies, he hit .370 in 1993 and drove in 150 runs in 1996.)
145. **A.** Frank Howard
   B. J.R. Richard
   C. Freddie Patek
   D. Jeff Juden
   E. Rafael Belliard
   F. Billy Taylor
146. John Olerud (He was traded from the Blue Jays to the Mets for Robert Person) and Paul O'Neill (He was traded from the Reds with Joe DeBerry to the Yankees for Roberto Kelly)
147. Roy Campanella (1953 Dodgers), Ted Kluszewski (1953, 1954, 1955 Reds), Carl Yastrzemski (1967, 1969, 1970 Red Sox), and Rico Petrocelli (1969 Red Sox)
148. 1. Guerrero (.300) 2. Lansford (.290) 3. Maddox (.285) 4. Cabell (.277) 5. Wilson (.274) 6. Braun (.271) 7. Rudi (.264) 8. Scioscia (.259) 9. Snyder (.247) 10. Mendoza (.215)
149. **A.** Al Downing
   B. Mickey Lolich
   C. Jim Palmer
   D. Wilbur Wood
150. Mel Ott (New York Giants, 1928-45)

BLAZING FASTBALLS
Who Am I?
151. Danny Jackson
152. Mickey Stanley
153. Tony Peña
154. Bob Tewksbury
155. Ruppert Jones
156. B.J. Surhoff
157. Kirk McCaskill
158. Gregg Jefferies
159. Dwight Smith
160. Shawon Dunston

161. Wally Backman
162. David West
163. Gregg Olson
164. Sid Bream
165. Scott Sanderson
166. Mariano Duncan
167. Joel Youngblood
168. Mike Morgan
169. Pete O'Brien
170. Bryan Harvey

Mixed Bag

171. **A.** Glenn Beckert
    B. Rowland Office
    C. Ken Landreaux
    D. Brian Harper
172. Rick Sutcliffe (1979)—Won ERA title for Tribe
    Steve Howe (1980)—Suspended six times
    Fernando Valenzuela (1981)—Sizzling start
    Steve Sax (1982)—1949 hits
    Eric Karros (1992)—Powerful first baseman
    Mike Piazza (1993)—Played for Dodgers, Marlins, and Mets in May 1998
    Raul Mondesi (1994)—Dominican Republic native
    Hideo Nomo (1995)—Held the Rockies hitless in 1996
    Todd Hollandsworth (1996)—Mediocre Rookie of the Year stats
173. Hansen—B
    Kittle—A
    Salmon—E
    Lynn—C
    Fisk—D
174. E. Ripken was named MVP of the 1991 All-Star Game; he was the American League's Rookie of the Year in 1982; he made just three errors in 1990; and he won the American League MVP in both the 1983 and 1991 seasons. He has never led the major league—or the American League—in home runs; 34 is his top mark (1991).
175. Ken (older) and Bob (younger) Forsch
176. Williams—A
    Murphy—D
    Mays—E
    Hernandez—B
    Aaron—C
177. 1982 Braves and 1987 Brewers

178.
   A. Tommy Greene
   B. Kevin Stocker
   C. Ricky Jordan
   D. Jim Eisenreich
   E. Milt Thompson
179. Sandberg—A
   Brock—D
   Otis—C
   Smith—E
   Nettles—B
180. Al Oliver hit .331 in 1982 at the age of 35 to win the title; he retired three years later. Tim Raines paced the National League with a .334 average in 1986; he picked up his 2500th hit for the Yankees in 1998. Pedro Martinez won the Cy Young Award in 1997 on the strength of a 1.90 ERA and 305 strikeouts; he signed with the Red Sox in the off-season, and won the Cy Young for them in 1999.
181.
   A. Joe Charboneau
   B. Orestes Destrade
   C. Buzz Capra
   D. Mike Norris
182.
   A. Boston Red Sox
   B. California Angels
   C. Milwaukee Brewers
   D. San Francisco Giants
183.
   A. Cliff Johnson
   B. Manny Mota
   C. John Vander Wal
   D. Del Unser
184. "Hurricane" Herb Washington and Matt Alexander
185.
   A. George "Doc" Medich
   B. Tony LaRussa
   C. Ron Darling
   D. Doug Glanville
186. Los Angeles Dodgers and San Francisco Giants. The Dodgers played .513 for the decade; they won the National League West in 1995, but got swept in the Division Series by the Reds and won the Wild Card berth in 1996, but the Braves took them out in three in the Division Series. The Giants' fortunes have been similar; they played .508 in the 1990s and were beaten

three games to none in 1997 by the Marlins after winning the National League West. You deserve honorable mention if you guessed the Expos; they never made it to the post-season in the '90s and finished a game below .500 (776–777).

187. **A.** Mickey Cochrane
   B. Dizzy Dean
   C. Herb Score
   D. Tony Conigliaro

188. Bobby Richardson's Yankees lost to the Pirates in the 1960 World Series.

189. A. Holtzman won Game 7 for the A's in 1973, Andujar for the Cardinals in 1982, Viola for the Twins in 1987, and Morris for the Twins in 1991. Holtzman pitched two no-hitters and Morris pitched one, but Andujar and Viola didn't throw one. Holtzman began and ended his career with the Cubs; ditto Andujar for the Astros (although they pitched for other teams in between). But Morris started with the Tigers and finished with the Indians, while Viola broke in with the Twins and finished with the Blue Jays. Viola pitched for the Red Sox; Holtzman pitched for the Yankees. Holtzman was 174–150, Viola 176–150, and Morris 254–186. Andujar fell short at 127–118.

190. Fabregas—E
   Pratt—C
   Petralli—A
   Wrona—B
   Servais—D

191. C. Kansas City/Oakland A's (1959–71)

192. **A.** 1971
   B. 1983
   C. 1967
   D. 1982
   E. 1995

193. Grove—C
   Gomez—D
   Leifield—A
   Williams—E
   Mills—B

194. B. Williams homered in the 1989 Series for the Giants and the 1997 Series for the Indians.

195. Mark Davis and Bobby Thigpen

196. D. Carter did not win a World Series MVP, nor did he win a league MVP. Hershiser won the World Series MVP in 1988, but did not win a league MVP. Foster did not win a World Series MVP, but won the N.L. MVP in 1977. Robinson won the A.L. MVP in 1964 and the World Series MVP in 1970. Bando did not win a World Series MVP, nor did he win a league MVP.

197. E. In 1986, Mitch appeared in 80 games for the Rangers to set the record for most games pitched by a rookie. The record was broken in 1996 when Tigers rookie Mike Myers pitched in 83 games. Two years later, another Tigers rookie, Sean Runyan, broke the record by making 88 appearances. In 1991 for the Phillies, Mitch won eight games in the month of August to set the record for the most wins by a reliever in a month. That record still stands.

198. Martin managed the Twins (1969), Tigers (1971–73), Rangers (1973–75), and A's (1980–82). He won division titles for the Twins (1969), Tigers (1972), and A's (1981), and finished second for the Rangers in 1974 after they lost 105 games in 1973. (He managed the last 23 games that year.)

199.   **A.** Brian Downing (282)
   B. Frank Thomas (301 through 1999)
   C. Robin Yount (2182)
   D. Lou Gehrig (163)
   E. Tony Fernandez (287 through 1999)
   F. Jose Cruz (80)
   G. Duke Snider (389)
   H. Tim Wallach (360)
   I. Mookie Wilson (62)
   J. Richie Ashburn (1811)

200. 1973 New York Mets

ABOUT THE AUTHORS

Mitch "The Wild Thing" Williams was a relief pitcher in the major leagues for 11 years. He lives in Texas with his wife Irene and their three children, Damon, Mitch Jr., and Nikola.

When he was growing up, Dave "The Mild Thing" Brown longed to be a sportswriter or baseball player, but somehow he got off the track and ended up as a lawyer. In between suing and getting sued, Dave has found time to fulfill his childhood aspirations: For years, he contributed articles to the "Numbers" and "Inside Out" columns of *Inside Sports* magazine, and last year he finished playing his ninth season in a slow-pitch, co-ed softball league in which he solidified his reputation as a fair-hitting, erratic-fielding pitcher/first baseman with no speed. He lives in the Philadelphia suburb of Wayne with his cat.

Index

A
Aaron, Hank, 70, 97, 119, 121
Ainge, Danny, 27, 112
Alexander, Doyle, 45, 114
Alexander, Matt, 101, 122
Allen, Dick, 69, 118
Alomar, Sandy, 50, 70, 116, 118
Alou, Filipe, 29, 113
Alou, Moises, 52–53, 117
Alston, Walter, 49, 115
Altobelli, Joe, 77, 120
Anderson, Brady, 63–64, 118
Anderson, Larry, 56, 117
Andujar, Joaquin, 104, 123
Angels, 54, 117
Aparicio, Luis, 26, 73, 112, 119
Armas, Tony, 30, 113
Ashburn, Richie, 28, 67, 108, 118, 124
Assenmacher, Paul, 47, 115
Atlanta Braves, 26, 97, 112, 121

B
Backman, Wally, 88, 121
Baerga, Carlos, 50, 116
Bagwell, Jeff, 18, 110
Baines, Harold, 32, 50, 113, 116
Baltimore Orioles, 26, 112
Banks, Ernie, 20, 44, 110, 114
Barker, Len, 75, 119
Barry, Hallie, 75, 119
Beckert, Glenn, 95, 121
Bedrosian, Steve, 49, 115
Belanger, Mark, 74–75, 119
Bell, Buddy, 53, 117
Bell, George, 36, 113
Belle, Albert, 48, 50, 115, 116
Belliard, Rafael, 78, 120
Bench, Johnny, 22–23, 111
Berra, Yogi, 25, 44, 112, 114
Blowers, Mike, 53, 117
Blue Jays, 54, 117
Blue, Vida, 51, 105, 116, 123
Blyleven, Bert, 19, 110
Boddicker, Mike, 50–51, 116
Boggs, Wade, 17, 50, 110, 116
Bonds, Barry, 32, 44, 113
Bonds, Bobby, 14, 110
Bonilla, Bobby, 41, 50, 52–53, 114, 116, 117
Boone, Bob, 70, 118
Boston Red Sox, 100, 122
Boston, Massachussets, 32, 113
Bouton, Jim, 24, 111
Boyer, Ken, 69, 118
Bradshaw, Terry, 46–47, 115
Braun, Steve, 79, 120
Braves, 26, 97, 112, 121
Bream, Sid, 90, 121

Brett, George, 13–14, 110
Brinkman, Eddie, 74–75, 119
Brock, Lou, 98, 122
Brooklyn Dodgers, 26, 30, 112, 113
Brown, Chris, 44, 114
Brown, Gates, 44, 114
Brown, Kevin, 44, 52–53, 114, 117
Brown, Ollie, 44, 114
Browning, Tom, 75, 119
Buechele, Steve, 61, 118
Bunning, Jim, 26, 112
Burdette, Lew, 31–32, 113
Burroughs, Jeff, 22

C
Cabell, Enos, 79, 120
California Angels, 54, 100, 117, 122
Campanella, Roy, 26, 79, 112, 120
Candelaria, John, 57, 117
Cangelosi, John, 50, 116
Capra, Buzz, 99, 122
Cardinals, 26, 30, 112, 113
Carew, Rod, 28–29, 51, 112, 116
Carlton, Steve, 28, 68, 118
Carter, Gary, 51, 107, 116, 124
Cepeda, Orlando, 22, 32, 110–111, 113
Cerone, Rick, 72, 119
Cey, Ron, 20–21, 110
Charboneau, Joe, 99, 122
Chicago Cubs, 22, 30, 110, 113
Chicago White Sox, 32, 113
Cincinnati Reds, 22, 26, 27, 110, 112, 112
Clark, Jack, 42–43, 114
Clark, Will "The Thrill," 16, 110
Clark, Willie, 32, 113
Clemens, Roger, 50, 51, 116, 116–117
Clemente, Roberto, 22–23, 28–29, 111, 112
Cleveland Indians, 22, 110
Cloninger, Tony, 72–73, 119
Cobb, Ty, 20, 53–54, 117
Cochrane, Mickey, 103, 123
Coleman, Vince, 73, 119
Collins, Terry, 44, 114
Concepcion, Dave, 24, 105, 111, 123
Cone, David, 75, 76–77, 119, 120
Conigliaro, Tony, 103, 123
Conine, Jeff, 105, 123
Conseco, Jose, 13, 110
Cooper, Gary, 46–47, 115
Craig, Roger, 67, 118
Cruz, Jose, 69, 108, 118, 124
Cubs, 22, 30, 110, 113

D
Dahlgren, Babe, 72, 119

Darling, Ron, 53, 102, 117, 122
Davis, Chili, 53, 117
Davis, Mark, 106–107, 123
Dawson, Andre, 20–21, 51, 110, 116
Dean, Dizzy, 103, 123
DeBusschere, Dave, 27, 112
DeCinces, Doug, 72, 119
Destrade, Orestes, 99, 122
Detroit Tigers, 30, 113
Dibble, Rob, 60–61, 117
DiMaggio, Joe, 69, 118
Dodgers
  Brooklyn, 26, 30, 112, 113
  Los Angeles, 30, 102, 113, 122–123
Donora, Pennsylvania, 28, 112
Downing, Al, 80–81, 120
Downing, Brian, 108, 124
Drysdale, Don, 15, 110
Duncan, Mariano, 91, 121
Dunston, Shawon, 87–88, 120
Dykstra, Lenny, 29, 38, 112, 114

E
Eisenreich, Jim, 52–53, 98, 117, 122
Evans, Darrell, 36–37, 113
Evans, Dwight, 42, 114
Expos, 54, 102, 117, 122–123

F
Fabregas, Jorge, 104, 123
Face, Elroy, 25, 111
Feller, Bob, 48–49, 115
Fernandez, Tony, 108, 124
Fidrych, Mark, 20–21, 110
Finley, Charley, 105, 123
Fisk, Carlton, 96, 121
Fletcher, Scott, 68, 118
Flood, Curt, 16–17, 110
Ford, Whitey, 20
Forsch, Bob, 97, 121
Forsch, Ken, 97, 121
Foster, George, 52, 117
Foxx, Jimmie, 20, 44, 114
Franchise moves, 46, 115
Franco, John, 35, 113
Francona, Terry, 27, 112
Fregosi, Jim, 44, 114

G
Galarraga, Andres, 77, 120
Garner, Phil, 29, 113
Garr, Ralph, 68, 118
Garvey, Steve, 22, 110
Gaston, Cito, 77, 120
Gehrig, Lou, 108, 124
Giants, 100, 102, 122, 122–123
Gibson, Bob, 68, 118
Gibson, Kirk, 39, 114
Girardi, Joe, 55, 117
Giusti, Dave, 25, 111
Glanville, Doug, 102, 122

Golden Gloves award, 22–23
Gomez, Lefty, 106, 123
Gooden, Dwight, 15, 110
Grace, Mark, 32–33, 113
Green, Dallas, 77, 120
Greene, Tommy, 98, 122
Griffey, Ken, 28, 112
Griffey, Ken Jr., 22–23, 28, 111, 112
Grove, Lefty, 106, 123
Guerrero, Pedro, 79, 120
Guidry, Ron, 24, 111
Guillen, Ozzie, 50, 116
H
Hairston, Sam, 70, 118
Hansen, Ron, 96, 121
Harper, Brian, 95, 121
Harrah, Toby, 68, 118
Harrleson, Bud, 74–75, 119
Harvey, Bryan, 93–94, 121
Hayes, Von, 51, 116
Henderson, Rickey, 71, 119
Hendrick, George, 30, 113
Hernandez, Keith, 22–23, 71, 97, 111, 119, 121
Hernandez, Willie, 22
Herschiser, Orel, 20–21, 110
Holland, Al, 49, 115
Hollandsworth, Todd, 95–96, 121
Hollins, Dave, 62–63, 118
Holtzman, Ken, 104, 123
Hornsby, Rogers, 52
Hough, Charlie, 40–41, 114
Houston Astros, 45, 114
Howard, Frank, 78, 120
Howe, Art, 29, 113
Howe, Steve, 95–96, 121
Howser, Dick, 77, 120
Hrbek, Kent, 64, 118
Hunter, Catfish, 26, 112
Hurst, Bruce, 50–51, 116
I
Incaviglia, Pete, 58–59, 117
J
Jackson, Bo, 36, 113
Jackson, Danny, 82, 120
Jackson, Michael, 46–47, 115
Jackson, Reggie, 20, 26, 52, 70, 112, 117, 119
Jefferies, Gregg, 86, 120
Jenkins, Ferguson, 30–31, 51, 113, 116
John, Tommy, 30–31, 113
Johnson, Charles, 52–53, 117
Johnson, Cliff, 100–101, 122
Johnson, Davey, 29, 113
Johnson, Howard, 39, 114
Johnson, Walter, 52
Johnstone, Jay, 24, 111
Jones, Rupert, 84, 120
Jordan, Ricky, 98, 122

Juden, Jeff, 78, 120
Justice, David, 75, 119
K
Kaat, Jim, 22–23, 111
Kaline, Al, 22–23, 111
Karros, Eric, 95–96, 121
Kennedy, Terry, 50–51, 116
Killebrew, Harmon, 26, 112
Kiner, Ralph, 74, 119
King, Billie Jean, 75, 119
Kingman, Dave, 76–77, 120
Kittle, Ron, 96, 121
Klein, Chuck, 48, 115
Kluszewski, Ted, 79, 120
Knight, Ray, 75, 119
Knoblauch, Chuck, 51, 116
Konstanty, Jim, 49, 115
Koosman, Jerry, 30–31, 113
Kruk, John, 33, 113
L
Lachemann, Marcel, 44, 114
Lahti, Christine, 75, 119
Lahti, Jeff, 75, 119
Landreaux, Ken, 95, 121
Lanier, Hal, 74–75, 119
Lansford, Carney, 79, 120
Larkin, Barry, 15, 110
Larsen, Don, 31–32, 113
LaRussa, Tony, 29, 102, 122
Lasorda, Tommy, 29, 49, 115
Leifield, Lefty, 106, 123
Leiter, Al, 52–53, 117
Lemon, Bob, 31–32, 113
Leyland, Jim, 29
Linz, Phil, 76–77, 120
Lofton, Kenny, 50, 116
Lolich, Mickey, 80–81, 120
Lopez, Nancy, 75, 119
Los Angeles Dodgers, 30, 102, 113, 122–123
Lyle, Sparky, 24, 111
Lynn, Fred, 96, 105, 121, 123
M
McCaskill, Kirk, 85–86, 120
McCovey, Willie, 22, 32, 110–111, 113
McGraw, Tug, 25, 49, 111, 115
McGregor, Scott, 24, 111
McGriff, Fred, 35, 113
McGwire, Mark, 13, 20, 68–69, 110
Maddox, Garry, 79, 120
Maddux, Greg, 47, 51, 115, 116–117
Maddux, Mike, 59–60, 117
Managers, 29, 44, 113, 114. *See also specific managers*.
Mantle, Mickey, 20, 44, 70, 110, 114, 119
Marichal, Juan, 51, 116
Mariners, 54, 117

Maris, Roger, 44, 69, 114, 118
Marlins, 22, 110
Marshall, Mike, 74, 119
Marshall, Peter, 75, 119
Martin, Billy, 108, 124
Martinez, Dennis, 18, 75, 110, 119
Martinez, Pedro, 99, 122
Matthews, Gary, 30, 113
Mattingly, Don, 24, 24, 111
Mauch, Gene, 28, 112
May, Derrick, 47, 115
Mays, Willie, 20, 22–23, 97, 111, 121
Medich, George "Doc," 102, 122
Mendoza, Mario, 79, 120
Mets, 22, 108–109, 110, 124
Mills, Lefty, 106, 123
Milwaukee Brewers, 100, 122
Minnesota Twins, 22, 110
Mitchell, Kevin, 22, 32, 113
Moffit, Randy, 75, 119
Molitor, Paul, 26, 112
Mondesi, Raul, 95–96, 121
Montreal Expos, 54, 102, 117, 122–123
Morgan, Joe, 44, 71, 73, 114, 119
Morgan, Mike, 92, 121
Morris, Jack, 45, 104, 115, 123
Mota, Manny, 70, 100–101, 118, 122
Murphy, Dale, 44, 97, 114, 121
Murray, Eddie, 20, 22, 26, 50, 110–111, 112, 116
Musial, Stan, 13, 28, 112
N
Nenn, Robb, 52–53, 117
Nettles, Graig, 98, 122
New York Mets, 22, 108–109, 110, 124
New York Yankees, 26, 112
Newhouser, Hal, 44, 114
Niekro, Joe, 30–31, 113
Niekro, Phil, 26, 51, 112, 116
Nilsson, Dave, 53, 117
Nomo, Hideo, 95–96, 121
Norris, Mike, 99, 122
O
O'Brien, Pete, 92–93, 121
O'Neill, Paul, 78–79, 120
Office, Rowland, 95, 121
Olerud, John, 78–79, 120
Oliver, Al, 99, 122
Olson, Gregg, 89–90, 121
Orioles, 26, 112
Orosco, Jesse, 50, 116
Otis, Amos, 98, 122
Ott, Mel, 20, 81, 110, 120
P
Paciorek, Tom, 68, 118
Padres, 22, 110

Palmer, Jim, 26, 68, 80–81, 112, 118, 120
Parker, Dave, 20–21, 110
Patek, Freddie, 78, 120
Peña, Tony, 83, 120
Pepitone, Joe, 24, 111
Perez, Tony, 18, 105, 110, 123
Perry, Gaylord, 24, 51, 111, 116
Perry, Jim, 51, 116
Petralli, Geno, 104, 123
Petrocelli, Rico, 79, 120
Pettitte, Andy, 45, 115
Philadelphia Phillies, 22, 30, 113
Piazza, Mike, 19, 95–96, 110, 121
Pittsburgh Pirates, 23, 51, 57, 69, 111, 116, 123
Porter, Darrell, 65, 118
Pratt, Todd, 104, 123
Puckett, Kirby, 14, 110

R

Raines, Tim, 99, 122
Ramirez, Manny, 50, 116
Reds, 22, 26, 27, 110, 112, 123
Reed, Ron, 27, 112
Retired numbers, 28–29, 112
Reuss, Jerry, 30–31, 113
Rice, Jim, 22, -111, 110
Richard, J.R., 78, 120
Richardson, Bobby, 104, 123
Rijo, Jose, 57–58, 117
Ripken, Cal Jr., 22, 70, 96, 119, 121
Rizzuto, Phil, 26, 112
Roberts, Robin, 28
Robinson, Brooks, 22–23, 70, 111, 119
Robinson, Frank, 20
Rodriguez, Ivan, 39, 114
Rogers, Kenny, 46–47, 75, 115, 119
Rogers, Steve, 105, 123
Rudi, Joe, 79, 120
Ruth, George Herman "Babe," 23, 68–69, 111
Ryan, Nolan, 48–49, 68, 115, 118

S

St. Louis Cardinals, 26, 30, 112, 113
Salazar, Luis, 47, 115
Salmon, Tim, 96, 121
San Diego Padres, 22, 110
San Francisco Giants, 100, 102, 122, 122–123
Sandberg, Ryne, 22–23, 71, 98, 111, 119, 122
Sanders, Deion, 15–16, 110
Sanderson, Scott, 90–91, 121
Sax, Steve, 95–96, 121
Schilling, Curt, 45, 53, 115, 117
Schiraldi, Calvin, 47, 115
Schmidt, Mike, 20, 28, 44, 110, 114

Scioscia, Mike, 79, 120
Score, Herb, 103, 123
Seattle Mariners, 54, 117
Seattle Pilots, 46, 115
Seaver, Tom, 50, 116
Senators, 54, 117
Servais, Scott, 104, 123
Sheffield, Gary, 52–53, 117
Sierra, Ruben, 56–57, 117
Simmons, Ted, 40, 114
Slaught, Don, 55, 117
Smith, Dwight, 86–87, 120
Smith, Lee, 19, 110
Smith, Ozzie, 17, 22–23, 98, 110, 111, 122
Smoltz, John, 45, 114
Snider, Duke, 108, 124
Snyder, Cory, 79, 120
Spahn, Warren, 28–29, 112
Splittorff, Paul, 24, 111
Stanley, Mickey, 82, 120
Stargell, Willie, 26, 112
Staub, Rusty, 47, 115
Stengel, Casey, 28–29, 112
Stewart, Dave, 35, 113
Stocker, Kevin, 98, 122
Stone, Steve, 70, 118
Stottlemyre, Mel, 70, 118
Strawberry, Darryl, 50, 76–77, 116, 120
Sucliffe, Rick, 65–66, 118
Sunberg, Jim, 68, 118
Surhoff, B.J., 84–85, 120
Sutcliffe, Rick, 95–96, 121
Sutter, Bruce, 25, 111
Sutton, Don, 68, 118

T

Tanana, Frank, 41, 114
Tanner, Chuck, 54, 117
Tartabull, Danny, 63, 118
Taylor, Billy, 78, 120
Tekulve, Kent, 74, 119
Tenace, Gene, 30, 113
Tettleton, Mickey, 62, 118
Tewksbury, Bob, 83–84, 120
Thigpen, Bobby, 106–107, 123
Thomas, Frank E., 44, 108, 124
Thomas, Frank J., 67, 118
Thome, Jim, 50, 58, 116, 117
Thompson, Milt, 98, 122
Thomson, Bobby, 31–32, 113
Thorneberry, Marv, 67, 118
Tiant, Luis, 51, 116
Tigers, 30, 113
Toronto Blue Jays, 54, 117
Torre, Joe, 29, 113
Torrez, Mike, 48–49, 115
Trades, 45, 51, 114, 116
Tudor, John, 65, 118

U

Unser, Del, 100–101, 122

V

Valentine, Bobby, 44, 114
Valentine, Ellis, 50–51, 116
Valenzuela, Fernando, 95–96, 121
Van Slyke, Andy, 50–51, 116
Vander Wal, John, 100–101, 122
Ventura, Robin, 61, 118
Viola, Frank, 104, 123

W

Walker, Larry, 37, 113
Wallach, Tim, 108, 124
Ward, Gary, 68, 118
Washington Senators, 54, 117
Washington, "Hurricane" Herb, 101, 122
Webb, Earl, 71, 119
Wells, David, 75, 119
West, David, 89, 121
Whitaker, Lou, 24, 111
White Sox, 32, 113
White, Devon, 52–53, 117
Wilhelm, Hoyt, 25, 111
Williams, Bernie, 44, 114
Williams, Billy, 22, 97, 110, 121
Williams, Charlie, 44, 114
Williams, Lefty, 106, 123
Williams, Matt, 32, 106, 113, 123
Williams, Mitch "The Wild Thing," 7, 9–12, 20, 29, 44, 68–69, 107, 110, 112, 114, 118, 124
Williams, Ted, 20, 44, 110, 114
Williams, Walt, 44, 114
Wills, Maury, 73, 119
Wilson, Don, 28–29, 112
Wilson, Mookie, 79, 108, 120, 124
Wilson, Owen "Chief," 71, 119
Wilson, Willie, 71, 73, 119, 119
Wine, Bud, 74–75, 119
Winfield, Dave, 16, 51, 110, 116
Wise, Rick, 48, 115
Witt, Bobby, 48–49, 115
Witt, Mike, 75, 119
Wood, Wilbur, 80–81, 120
Wrona, Rick, 104, 123
Wynn, Early, 31–32, 113

Y

Yankees, 26, 112
Yastrzemski, Carl, 31, 72, 79, 113, 119, 120
Young, Cy, 99, 122
Youngblood, Joel, 92, 121
Yount, Robin, 13, 22, 51, 108, 110–111, 116, 124

Z

Zimmer, Don, 44, 114
Zisk, Richie, 30, 113